John Percival Jones

The Optional Standard

A Speech Delivered in the Senate of the United States...

John Percival Jones

The Optional Standard
A Speech Delivered in the Senate of the United States...

ISBN/EAN: 9783337151461

Printed in Europe, USA, Canada, Australia, Japan

Cover: Foto ©Suzi / pixelio.de

More available books at **www.hansebooks.com**

THE OPTIONAL STANDARD,

A SPEECH DELIVERED IN THE SENATE OF
THE UNITED STATES, JUNE 28, 1876;

ALSO

THE CONFERENCE REPORT ON SILVER,

A SPEECH DELIVERED IN THE SENATE OF THE
UNITED STATES, JULY 15, 1876.

BY

JOHN P. JONES,

SENATOR FROM NEVADA.

———◆———

WASHINGTON.
1876.

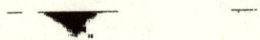

THE OPTIONAL STANDARD,

A SPEECH DELIVERED IN THE SENATE OF THE UNITED
STATES, JUNE 28, 1876,

BY

JOHN P. JONES,

SENATOR FROM NEVADA.

The Senate, as in Committee of the Whole, having under consideration the bill
(H. R. No. 3398) for the issue of coin, and for other purposes, the following pro-
ceedings occurred·

Mr. JONES, of Nevada. Mr. President, I desire to offer an amendment to the bill.

The PRESIDING OFFICER, (Mr. WHYTE in the chair.) The Secretary will report the proposed amendment.

The CHIEF CLERK. It is proposed to amend the first section by
striking out lines 13, 14, 15, 16, and 17, and inserting in lieu thereof :

And the said dollar herein authorized shall be a legal tender at its nominal value
for any and all amounts, except for customs duties, and for debts and obligations
which by their own terms are payable in gold coin.

It is further proposed to insert as section 5 :

That any owner of silver bullion may deposit the same at any mint to be formed,
for his benefit, into silver dollars such as are provided for in this act, or into bars ;
and the charge for such manufacture shall not exceed the actual cost thereof as
may be computed by the Director of the Mint and approved by the Secretary of
the Treasury.

The PRESIDING OFFICER. The amendment of the Senator from
Nevada is not now in order. It has been read for information. There
are two prior amendments already pending.

Mr. JONES, of Nevada. I shall address myself, the same as though
it were in order, to the amendment just read, which I shall offer at
the proper time.

REPLIES TO SENATOR BOOTH'S OBJECTIONS.

In the remarks which I propose to submit to the Senate, I shall endeavor to confine myself to the bill now under discussion, and to the
observations that have been made relative to the subject by those
who have preceded me. With these objects immediately in view, I

shall not digress to discuss new systems of fiat paper money, nor to dis
cover inconsistencies or errors of phraseology in the old and forgotten
speeches of my colleagues.

In the exceedingly interesting and able speech of the Senator from
California, [Mr. Booth,] he lays down several propositions, among
which are the following:

First. That silver has been, during the past few years, as variable
in value as United States notes.

To this I reply that United States notes have insensibly, though
incorrectly, been regarded as promises to pay gold ; this regard having been fastened upon them by the fact that, until 1873, the gold
dollar was less valuable than the silver dollar, and therefore was the
only current coin, and that since 1873 the silver dollar has been demonetized. That being thus regarded as promises to pay gold, United States
notes have followed gold, and fluctuated with it, while silver has remained nearly stationary. As gold and greenbacks are not custom-
arily quoted in silver, but, on the contrary, silver is quoted in gold
and greenbacks, silver has appeared to greatly fluctuate in value,
whereas, in point of fact, it has fluctuated very little ; and the Senator has no right to assume that it has fluctuated more than either
gold or greenbacks.

Second. That silver would be too heavy to carry in the pocket.

To this I reply that so is gold, and that neither, in case of a silver,
a gold, or a double standard of money, would coin be carried in the
pocket to more than a very small amount. Government certificates
for deposits of coin in money in note-form, or bank-notes, based on a
deposit of coin, would be chiefly used, and would furnish the people
a safe and convenient medium of exchange and at the same time prevent all loss from abrasion of metal money. The Senator himself says
a little further on—

The superior convenience of paper money will prevent the extensive circulation
of silver.

Third. That we parted with the silver dollar twenty-three years
ago.

In this he is mistaken. We parted with it forty-two years ago, or
in 1834, because in that year a legal relation was established between
the two metals, which overvalued gold and undervalued silver. The
silver dollar, being the more valuable of the two in the market, was
exported ; but we retained the silver dollar as legal money for any
and all purposes, and had and held the valuable option of again coining it in case there should occur what has recently occurred: a rise in
the price of gold or a decline in the value of silver.

Fourth. The Senator says that no living man has the courage to
face the consequences of specie payments.

Now if specie payments, to be made in gold, are so alarming, why does the Senator argue in opposition to specie payments in silver, which, according to his own statement, would bo 20 per cent. easier?

Fifth. That it is the true policy to bring every form of currency to the gold standard, because that is the one used by the commercial world.

I have heretofore shown that, of all the nations in the commercial world, only England and her *protégés*, Turkey, Portugal, Brazil, and Chili, employ the single gold standard. All the rest use either the double or the single silver standard. But it is not the gold standard alone which the gentleman advocates; it is a gold standard and a particular unit of value in that standard coupled with it. It is a gold standard with 23.22 grains of pure gold in each unit called a dollar; a unit 15 per cent. above the value of the currency unit, under which nearly all contracts now in existence in this country have been entered into, and under which, since 1862, all the promissory notes and mortgages have been executed and obligations incurred.

Even admitting that the bonds of the Government should be paid in gold, he would, merely for the sake of harmony in nomenclature, add 15 per cent. in weight to the burden of debts in this land by making all of them, municipal, State, and individual, amounting to several thousands of millions of dollars, in currency, payable, each dollar, by precisely the same weight of metal which he believes to be due to the foreign creditors of the Government.

Sixth. That the words "market value," as used in the bill under discussion, have no meaning if the silver bullion purchased in pursuance of its provisions is measured in silver dollars, because, as he says, to quote silver in itself would be absurd. It seems strange to me that this should strike any one as absurd. I ask him how does England value gold bullion when she purchases it for her mint at £3 17s. 10¼d. sterling per ounce? Not in silver, nor in wheat, neither of which are money in England, but in pieces of gold of standard purity, weighing a certain number of grains, and called pounds or sovereigns.

I give the latest quotations from the London Economist:

Quotations for bullion. Gold: Bar gold, 77s. 9d. per ounce standard; fine, 77s, 9d. per ounce standard; refinable, 77s. 11d. per ounce standard; United States gold coin, 76s. 3½d. per ounce; German gold coin, 76s 3½d. per ounce. Silver: Bar silver, fine, 51½d. per ounce standard, nearest; containing five grains gold, 52⁹/₁₆d. per ounce standard, nearest; Spanish dollars, (Carolus,) none here.

In like manner the silver bullion to be purchased under the provisions of this bill may be quoted in and paid for with silver pieces, each of which contains a specified number of grains of standard silver and is called a dollar. If this is impracticable, I have only to say that the world seems not to have discovered the fact; for it has pursued precisely this course ever since mints were established, many centuries ago.

Seventh. That he fails to perceive the important consequences which were attributed by me to the omission to provide for the coinage of the silver dollar in 1873, and that he has always consoled himself with the reflection that the mighty stream of human life would flow on in its great channel despite any accidental mistake of ours. I can scarcely believe that the Senator is so unmindful, as this extract would seem to make him out to be, of the mighty influence which, in all ages, legislation has had on the happiness, the material, moral, and social advancement of the human race. His argument would belittle all legislation. Was the recognition, in the Constitution and laws of the country of the right to hold human beings as property, of no import? Did not the results which flowed directly from these laws, and which are yet fresh in our memories, cause the mighty stream of human life to swerve from its natural channel? Are our laws guaranteeing personal freedom of no account? Are the national debt and the debts of individuals and corporations, all of which rest upon legislation, which, withdrawn, would occasion a redistribution of poverty and wealth in this country, of no account? And is an enactment which threatens to add 20 per cent. to the huge national debt and to the still greater State, municipal, and private debts of this country, and in that ratio increase the burdens of taxation, a mere accidental mistake not worthy of notice? The mighty stream of life to which the Senator alludes might continue to flow on, and I trust it will; but in the absence of wise legislation I fear that its flow would be over a very rocky bottom, and that its surface would not be so placid and smooth as might be wished.

Eighth. The Senator alleges that inasmuch as the entire coinage of silver in the mints of the United States from 1821 to 1873 was but $140,000,000 the disturbance caused by the act of 1873 is imaginary, Without commenting upon the incompleteness of the Senator's figures. for we coined silver previous to 1821, it needs only to be said that from 1834 to 1873, or nearly the whole of the period covered by the Senator's figures, silver was undervalued by our mint laws and was worth more as bullion than the Mint was authorized to pay for it for the purposes of coinage. The silver dollar was worth more in the markets of the world than the gold dollar, and was consequently coined only in limited quantities.

This fact affords no grounds for assuming that its great fitness for money is imaginary, or that the option of coining it, which was taken away from us by the act of 1873, was not a very valuable one, and one which alone was adequate to protect this nation against the ultimately ruinous effects of that great rise in the value of gold which has been effected by foreign legislation, and against this country's interest, since that date.

Ninth. The Senator objects to the silver dollar on the ground that its substitution for the present greenback dollar would simply amount to the exchanging, at a large expense, of one system for another. Further on he indicates his preference for the gold dollar over the silver one, ignoring the fact that the expense in this case would be much greater. Still further on he advocates, if I understand him correctly, a legal-tender paper dollar convertible into gold-bearing bonds at the option of the holder.

Not knowing which of these various propositions the Senator would oppose to the one under consideration, I am at a loss to compare or contrast them, and so leave them to carry, each of them, what weight it will.

Tenth. That to start with one metal thirteen degrees below the other is simply to adopt the lower standard and to abandon the only benefit—mutual corrections and modifications in the value of the two metals—which it is claimed results from the employment of the double standard. This statement involves the assumption that the present market ratio of silver to gold is the correct or normal one, an assumption the fallacy of which is known of all men. I had supposed that the world's experience of nearly three hundred years, that the normal relation between the metals of 15½ in silver to 1 in gold, was of some value in this discussion, and not to be overturned by the short experience of three years under exceptional and abnormal conditions.

The Senator himself, in one part of his speech, grants my conclusions in this respect "to the full," but in another he undertakes to overthrow them entirely by assuming that the present abnormal ratio would continue to exist even after the principal cause of it, the demonetization of silver by a leading commercial nation, were removed; or, what is the same thing, after another nation of greater commercial importance should give it even greater employment; and the fact ought to be clearly understood and appreciated, that in the equalization of the values of the two metals by the monetization of silver the lowering of the price of gold which would result therefrom, would contribute fully as much to bring about that result as the increase in the value of silver.

Eleventh. That the option or right of election to pay our national debt in silver or gold at the relation of 16 to 1, as provided by the law as it stood when the debt was contracted, is purely technical.

This assertion of technicality the Senator himself refutes a little further on by saying that "this election has determined the market value or price of our bonds at home and abroad." If this be true, this determination could only have been of interest to our Government at the time of the sale of the bonds, for after a thing is sold the seller can have no further interest in it, unless it be to buy it back cheaply. If the option determined the price at that time, it must have been something more than a mere technicality.

It is doubtful to me whether anything but the consideration, that an annual interest, equal to about 12 per cent. on the then market value of the bonds, which was promised to be paid in coin out of the customs revenues, had any weight with the foreign money-lender; but this is of little consequence at the present time.

The Senator regards this option as a mere technicality; and yet, according to his own figures, it is now worth to us $300,000,000 in solid cash. He regards it as a mere technicality, and yet argues that we shall fail to acquire the good opinion of the world unless we give it up for nothing.

An opinion which is ready to lend itself for a valuable consideration can hardly be deemed an honest one, and when the price demanded is so extravagant as it is in this case, it may be well worth consideration whether, as a nation, we might not be able to survive without it.

But, as I said on a previous occasion, I do not propose in the discussion of the bill under consideration to especially consider the question whether the public debt is payable in silver dollars or not.

It is a trivial question compared with the one whether our State, municipal, corporative, and private indebtedness, which was contracted in depreciated paper money, shall be forced to be paid in gold dollars, which even now, when gold has not been increased in value by the demands for it for purposes of resumption, is fully 15 per cent. more valuable than the paper units in which these debts were contracted or in the silver dollars provided for in this bill with which the differences between debtor and creditor can be fairly adjusted.

It is to this overshadowing question of the general indebtedness of this country and the mad attempt to force its payment in a unit of value not calculated on when the debts were contracted and in a metal already scarce and which is daily becoming scarcer, that I am giving my attention, and not to the minor consideration of the national debt, nor that good opinion of the world of money-changers which is controlled by a money consideration. On this question I propose to say something more further on, and therefore in this place I merely reply to the honorable Senator from California that what he regards as only a technical option is of considerably more importance even than that which he admits it possessed, namely, the determination of the market value of our national bonds. Its importance is chiefly to be found in regard to the bearing it has upon the general currency indebtedness of the country, which in amount is many times that of the sum of national indebtedness, bonded or otherwise.

Twelfth. The gentleman summarizes his speech under six points;

the first of which is, that the funded debt of the Government should be paid in gold.

To this proposition I have only to say that, the legal right to pay in silver being admitted on all sides, I prefer to postpone the discussion of the policy of exercising that right, which is a question of greater range, to a future occasion.

His second proposition is that the double standard requires, at the time of its adoption, "a common unit of value," and to avail ourselves of its supposed benefits we must increase the weight of the silver dollar. To this proposition I propose now to reply more specifically.

HISTORY OF THE AMERICAN DOLLAR.

The facts are briefly these: For more than two hundred years, that is to say, since shortly after the discovery of America, the market ratio of silver and gold throughout the commercial world was, with slight variation, 15½ for 1; in other words, fifteen and a half pounds of pure silver was the equivalent of one pound of gold. About fifty years ago, England, a leading commercial nation, then having, by her law of 1798, a qualified double standard, but really having suspended specie payments, suddenly changed her law and made gold the only legal tender for payments above £2. Gold was at that time slightly cheaper than silver, at the long-time relation of 15½ for 1, and, in adopting gold as her standard, England adopted the then cheaper metal; and in so doing followed precisely the course which the Senator from California views in our case with so much apprehension for the honor of the country. The consequence of the rejection of silver in England and the establishment of gold as the only metal in which her vast commercial transactions should be settled, was, when she came to resume specie payments in 1821, a temporary and rapid appreciation of gold from less than 15½ to 1 to nearly 16 for 1. From this cause a new equivalent between the metals was temporarily substituted for the old one; and in order to retain in their laws such an average relation between the metals as the market now showed, the other nations of the world, most of whom employed the double standard, and such as did not employed the single silver standard, fixed the legal relation of gold to silver at 15½ to 1. This country changed the relation from 15 for 1 to about 16 for 1. This was an undervaluation of silver and caused its exportation. This law was passed in the United States in 1834, and the legal relation then established between the metals has remained unchanged upon our statute-books to the present time.

Lately Germany, now also a leading commercial nation, prepared to do just what England did in 1816, namely, change an unqualified double standard (England had an unqualified double standard from 1793 to 1798) to a single gold standard.

The consequences in this case have been similar to those which occurred in the case of England. The elimination of some two hundred and fifty or three hundred millions of dollars of silver from the currency of Germany and the substitution therefor of an equal sum of gold—most of which she had to go into the markets and purchase—has caused such a temporary change in the relative value of gold and silver that instead of fifteen and one-half it now requires over eighteen pounds of silver to purchase one of gold.

If all the rest of the commercial nations had been on a specie basis when Germany resolved, unwisely as I think, on this change, her surplus silver would have been readily absorbed, without making scarcely any change in the relation between the metals. But this was not the case. Specie payments were, and are now, suspended in the countries representing the larger portion of the population of Europe as well as in the United States. Consequently there was not then, and is not now but a limited demand for silver in the Occidental world, and the sluggishness of commercial movements in the Orient prevents the ready absorption of a large amount of their money metal suddenly thrown upon them. And it is worthy of special consideration, concerning the passage of the law of 1834, changing the relation of silver to gold from 15 for 1 to about 16 for 1, that, at the former relation, gold stood at about 6½ per cent. premium over silver. Both were a legal tender for all amounts, the same as currency and gold are to-day. Silver was then the currency of the country, because it was the cheaper money, and, as a consequence, drove gold from the circulation; just as our present currency, which is 15 per cent. less valuable than gold, has driven gold from the circulation.

In 1834 it was deemed desirable by leading financiers of the country to bring gold in as an element of the currency with silver, just as it is now proposed to bring gold in by equalizing the paper legal tender and gold dollars. But a very different and more equitable plan was adopted to effect that object then than is proposed for the same end now. Mr. Campbell White, the chairman of the Committee on Coins; Mr. Albert Gallatin, one of the most distinguished financiers of this or any other country, and a former Senator of the United States; and Mr. Ingham, the Secretary of the Treasury, in discussing the question, agreed, as did also the Congress of the United States, that, as all time-contracts and obligations were based on the cheaper silver unit, it would be an outrage and an injustice not to be thought of nor tolerated, to change the relation of silver to gold by increasing the value of the silver dollar. Aside from the weighty material interests involved in the changing of the very essence of all existing contracts it was contended that such a course would severely shock the keen moral sensibilities of the nation; it would be a lesson in fraud and dishonesty which it could not afford to inculcate, and that we should not permit the creditor by a trick of legislation to exact from the debtor 6¼ per cent. more than his just due. A sensible and honest course was resolved upon and pursued; a sufficient number of grains of pure gold was taken from the gold unit to equalize its value with the silver unit, which was that upon which business and contracts rested.

THE PRACTICAL QUESTION.

A similar equitable course is what should be pursued now. Contracts and obligations are now based upon the paper dollar just as they were then based upon the silver dollar. To raise the paper to the gold dollar of to-day would work double the injustice that could have been worked by raising the silver to the gold dollar in 1834; for the difference is now 15 per cent., whereas then it was but 6¼. The fraud would be double, the trick of legislation twice as atrocious. Now, as then, the sensible and honest course would be to reduce the gold dollar rather than raise the paper one; for the paper dollar and not the gold one is the dollar upon which all our business affairs, mortgages, and other contracts are based.

But there are always well-founded objections to the reduction of coins. Exceptional contracts are sometimes in existence based upon the especial coin to be changed; and the use of two kinds of coin of one metal and both with the same name might lead to confusion. A new coinage becomes requisite and the coinage of any large sum of bullion is always subject to some expense and often to great inconvenience; and future changes may occur in the market value of the rejected coin which may render its rehabilitation desirable.

These objections to following the example of our country in 1834 are happily all removed by restoring the silver dollar to free coinage and full legal tender, both of which attributes it possessed up to the year 1873-'74, when they were abolished by covert legislation.

The silver dollar of 371¼ grains pure, or 412.8 grains standard, is at the present time of about the same value as the paper dollar, and therefore will accurately measure the bargains and contracts made in the last-named currency.

To restore it to free coinage and legal tender is simply to place it where it stood from the time when the white man first trod this country down to the year 1873-'74. It is to place it where it should stand, the peer of the gold dollar, both of them legal tenders to any amount for the payment of debts, the option between them to pertain to the lender when he lends money and to the borrower when he pays it.

MONEY SYSTEMS MUST CONFORM TO HISTORICAL FACTS.

Nations must base their systems of money not upon theories which exclude practical facts, but upon theories which recognize them . They must be prepared to receive and utilize large supplies of specie from countries suspending specie payments, in order to counterbalance the losses they sustain when they are obliged to suspend specie payments themselves. They must be prepared to respond to sudden and great demands for specie from countries returning to specie payments, in order that by their profits from this source they may make good their losses upon the specie they may be at some other time obliged to purchase in order to return to specie payments themselves.

SUSPENSION OF SPECIE PAYMENTS.

The United States suspended specie payments in 1861, and disposed of all that portion of its stock of specie, amounting to over $100,000,000, which consisted of silver, besides more or less of its gold. Other countries, as Austria and Italy, also suspended some years afterward, and their silver stock was thrown upon the markets of the world, causing more or less perturbation in the purchasing power and relative value of the precious metals.

When it suspended specie payments, the United States was a nation of thirty-one millions, and had a double standard, with gold as the cheaper metal, and comparatively little silver in circulation. Now when it proposes to resume specie payments it is a nation of forty-five millions, and should have a double standard, with silver as the cheaper metal, and comparatively little gold. It requires a stock of specie of not less than three hundred and fifty millions, accordingly as it shall conclude to establish its standard, whether of gold or silver or both, and with or without qualification, and over or under the average market ratios between the metals. This sum will be more or less in gold or in silver. My own plan is simply that which was the law of this land from 1792 (as amended in 1834) to 1873, namely, the unqualified double standard at 16 for 1. I say unqualified, although since 1853 the fractional coins, halves, quarters, dimes, and half dimes have been debased. I propose no change in these at present. The adoption of this plan, which is to be effected by simply restoring the silver dollar to legal tender and free coinage, would involve the purchase by the Government of from one hundred millions to two hundred millions of dollars of silver wherewith to resume specie payments.

PROBABLE EFFECT OF RESUMING IN SILVER.

This purchase would, as I believe—and in this I am backed by all experience—have the effect of restoring the market relation of 16 for 1, and thus the market and the legal relation would become the same. The one hundred or two hundred millions thus purchased would take all or nearly all the silver that Germany has left, and would fully counteract the effect upon the market ratio which her attempted change of standard has thus far been chiefly instrumental in producing.

Thus we should start substantially as the Senator from California contends we ought to, at such a legal relation between silver and gold as corresponded, or as would soon correspond, with the market relation; and therefore it would not be necessary, even from his point of view, to change the relation from the old one of 16 for 1 to any other.

As for any apprehension that the product of the silver mines of this country would tend to keep the relation at above 15½ or 16, this is a mere chimera. I showed on a previous occasion that concurrently with the increased product of the Comstock lode there has been a diminished product from other mines, and I now unhesitatingly affirm that in all the United States there are not ten silver mines that are more than paying expenses, and that in no district outside of the Comstock, which is now being worked at a depth of twenty-four hundred feet, is there any profit in silver mining.

The world's total annual product of silver is actually a trifle less now than it was three years ago and but twice as great as it was a century ago. The total silver product of the world is now but seventy-two millions. It was seventy-six millions in 1873, and over thirty-five millions in 1790.

While silver has been produced in tolerably close correspondence with the world's population and with food and the other principal articles of subsistence, the production of gold has fluctuated enormously. Silver and other commodities have preserved an even relation, and a given quantity of one will exchange for about the same quantity of the other as it would do twenty-five years ago, whilst gold is becoming dearer in relation to other commodities from day to day.

GRESHAM'S LAW.

The Senator's third proposition is that "all forms of currency in use at any given time ought to be equivalent in value." To this proposition I assent; and I say more, that you cannot make them differ and remain current; for so soon as they differ, all but one of them, the cheapest, will cease to be current. An objection has been made that with the re-instatement of the silver dollar we should have three kinds of dollars in circulation of different values, each of them a legal tender for any amount, and that utter confusion in our monetary system would be the result. Such a conclusion is unwarranted, because the predicate is impossible. As fast as the silver dollar is coined and issued it will take the place of the paper dollar, and as between the silver and gold dollar the cheaper one will be used exclusively as a means of payment. Therefore only one will be employed. and no confusion could result..

GOLD NEITHER A COMMON NOR AN INVARIABLE STANDARD.

The fourth proposition of the Senator from California is that "gold by the common consent of the commercial world is the ultimate standard by which all values are measured." The Senator will, I think, pardon me if I say that this is a mere assumption without even the appearance of evidence to prove it. Gold is not the common standard of the commercial world, nor has it ever been, nor is it likely ever to be so. Gold is not mined; it is picked up. It is chiefly the product of placers. Its annual production varies even of late from one hundred and ninety-four millions a year in 1852 to ninety-seven millions a year in 1875. The entire stock on hand in the world scarcely exceeds that of silver. As a measure of value it lacks the stability, steadiness, and universal distribution of silver. Ten years ago 100 grains of it scarcely purchased a day's labor of a mechanic in this country. Now 50 grains or less will purchase that amount of labor. It is the same with commodities, and commodities not only in this country but all over the commercial world. While the gentleman is proclaiming gold to be a universal measure of value, the prices of commodities in gold throughout such portions of the commercial world where gold is employed as the standard, are rapidly falling, and bankruptcy and ruin stare the merchant in the face.

Where silver is employed this is not the case. The cries of distress which this condition of affairs produces appear to be unheard by the Senator; but, like Pharaoh of old, the progress of events will compel him at length to listen to the counsel of reason.

THE CREDIT SYSTEM.

That portion of the question which we are now considering, the part which relates to resumption in specie, must not be decided by the light of the past, for in the past the credit system had not become so extended as it is now. Credit has advanced with the security afforded by freedom and an impartial administration of justice. Less than a century ago almost the entire population of Europe were serfs, while judicial systems had scarcely more than taken form. Even fifty years ago a proposition to appreciate the standard would have but little affected the public interest; whilst now it threatens the entire relations of society. There was scarcely any international debt at that time, but little public debt, and no great amount of private debt. The corporate system was in its birth, and great corporations and corporative debts were almost unknown. To increase the weight of debt by enhancing the standard was never so serious a question as it is now, and the country will weigh our deliberations on this topic with a criticism which is sharpened by the gravest apprehensions.

With the advance which society has made during the past century there have come into the arena of financial discussion, questions which were so foreign to them a century ago that when Adam Smith wrote his Wealth of Nations he gave no place to them in his book, but published a separate work on these considerations. The moral qualities had then no commercial standing. There was no market value to enterprise, perseverance, integrity, frugality, and virtue. Now they are quoted in the mercantile-agency reports to the *finesse* of fractions. The credit system has grown up in their sunshine and upon this system rest the most important institutions of modern society. Yet this system you coldly propose to destroy by chaining it to a single metal, already monopolized and scarce, whose production is governed by chance and whose annual yield is diminishing. Should you effect this rash and ill-considered purpose, who would care hereafter to trust or to be trusted, to give credit or to ask for it? What would become of long leases, long bonds, or any permanent form of credit? Who would bargain to borrow dollars or to get into debt for dollars, when their value might be doubled within a few years? Nobody. The credit system would crumble to the dust and the great moral qualities which have built it up would perish with it for want of recognition and reward. The miser would again hug his gold and the bold inventor and adventurer would languish for want of capital to carry out his ideas or recompense his efforts.

FORCED PAPER SCHEMES.

The Senator here leaves the subject of specie payments and ingeniously and ably expounds the merits of a credit currency based upon interconvertible bonds, with occasional glimpses of ultimate gold redemption, like a dissolving view, in the distance. This, with but slight surface variation, is an old scheme of credit, which has been tried in various forms in most of the countries of the world, and which, from inherent weakness, has invariably failed.

I am opposed to it and all other schemes for manufacturing money out of any material which would not be equally as valuable in the market, whether it had the Government stamp on it or not.

FREE MONEY.

In advocating the restoration of silver to the standard I wish it to be distinctly understood that I am not in favor of any debased coinage, neither is any one who has spoken or written in favor of bimetallic money. The money we propose to use is to be worth as coin no more than it is worth as bullion, excepting of course the slight cost of its manufacture. I advocate no violation of contracts; no interference with bargains; no raising or lowering of prices; no advantage to debtor or creditor. My judgment is opposed to all fiat paper money and all debased subsidiary metal money, unless the duty of redemption in full-weighted money is coupled with the authority to issue it. I believe in the necessity and advantage of using both the metals, silver and gold, as money. I believe in the right of any person to have his bullion, whether of gold or silver, coined at the national mints, at cost price, and returned to him in as many coins as can be made out of it. I believe in the propriety and advantage of unlimited legal tenders in regard to any and all of these coins, so long as they remain of full weight within the mint allowance of remedy. I believe that the day of seigniorage and royalties has passed, and that the money of this country, like its institutions, ought to be free. I do not propose any benefit for myself or for the gold and silver miners, or for any class of persons or corporations or things.

I propose simply that the Government, which has wisely reserved to itself the monopoly of coinage, shall conduct that monopoly in the interest of the people who authorized it, and by supplying them at the cost of manufacture with all the coins for which they deposit bullion, weight for weight.

The plan I would adopt has no limitations or restrictions about it ; no artificial arrangements ; no bounds, rivets, straps, or ligatures. It is the plan of simplicity and of justice ; justice to ourselves ; justice to debtor and creditor ; justice to all the world.

It is precisely the system which prevailed in this country from 1792 to 1853 ; a system which everybody understood and under which the United States grew and prospered from three millions to twenty-five millions of people, wealthy and powerful. It gives value for value, equivalent for equivalent, weight for weight. That is all there is about it.

IMPUTATIONS REPELLED.

And right here it may not be out of place to reply to those who have imputed my advocacy of a return to the double standard to unworthy motives, to my interests in silver mining.

The silver mines of Western Nevada yield almost as much gold as silver ; in fact, the ore contains about 45 per cent. of gold to 55 per cent. of silver. Hence those interested in them would, by the adoption of the double standard, make on the one hand but little more than they would lose on the other.

My own pecuniary interests in mines which yield gold to the entire exclusion of silver is far greater than my interests in silver mines, and consequently in advocating a return to the bimetallic standard I am really arguing against, instead of for, my own interests. None but those who are strangers to me have ever made the vulgar imputation. Yet, were it true, it could not weaken the force of the argument ; for the interests of an individual and the public may be, and often are, identical. But it is not true, nor could it be true.

The man who accepts a position of public trust and uses it either directly or indirectly for his own personal advantage, who subordinates public duty to private interests, who sells honor for profit, immediate or contingent, commits a crime so base and despicable that our language has no fitting name for it. Contrasted with it, bold theft becomes respectable and open treason honorable ; and whenever such an offense has been committed and the offender discovered, whether he be intrenched in powerful position or endowed with brilliant talents, if the country does not blast the offense and the offender with the mildew of its scórn, then indeed are our institutions in peril, greater peril than they could be subjected to from armed foes, however powerful, whether foreign or domestic.

REPLY TO SENATOR MORRILL.

I now turn to the speech of the distinguished Senator from Vermont. He began by quoting from my speech of April, 1874, in favor of resuming specie payments and against further continuance of our present irredeemable paper system, and appeared to suppose that he furnished an irresistible argument against the restoration of the bi-metallic standard when he quoted me as preferring gold to paper money some two years ago.

By what process of reasoning the Senator arrived at such a conclusion I am at a loss to conceive. I just as much prefer gold money to paper money to-day as I did two years ago, but that does not prevent me from also preferring in an equal degree silver money to paper. It has all the advantages that gold has and some that gold has not. The annual addition to the world's stock of silver is regular and moderate, because silver is the product of organized and competitive labor. The annual addition to the world's stock of gold is irregular, and, at the present time, insufficient. This irregularity and insufficiency result from the hap-hazard nature of gold-mining, which is chiefly in placers.

When I used the word "gold" in the speech referred to I used it as a generic term, meaning the precious metals, gold and silver, which I thought then and think now, and which the experience of the ages has demonstrated to be, the fittest material for the money of the world. I was not aware that the valuable option which the country had always enjoyed of using either gold or silver as unlimited legal tender had been abolished by the mint law of 1873.

If the Senator who deems it essential to the merits of this question to ascertain whether my views upon the subject have always been consistent will simply substitute the words "precious metals" for the word "gold" in my speech of 1874 I think he will find nothing to carp at. Not that I regard a man's consistency as a just criterion of the soundness of his latest views, for it is better to be right, even though once wrong, than to remain wrong for fear of the charge of inconsistency. But such a charge has but narrow ground to stand upon when it rests only upon the use of the term "gold" in the place of "precious metals."

Addressing himself to the merits of the bill before us, the Senator characterizes the dollar of 1792, which he appears to erroneously suppose was originated in 1837, as "a degraded dollar," and that its further coinage would "revolutionize the policy and traditions of the American people."

This is very extraordinary language from one who was a member of the legislative body which suppressed the coinage of that dollar only three years ago and after it had been in continuous use in this country, not merely since 1792, but from the time of the conquest of Peru by Francisco Pizarro; for the American silver dollar of 1792 was the same in weight of pure metal as the Spanish dollar and was copied after that coin by Alexander Hamilton, who had a number of Spanish dollars, as he found them in circulation, assayed for that purpose.

HISTORY OF THE AMERICAN DOLLAR.

It is only necessary to state the motive with which Hamilton caused this assay to be made and the Spanish dollar to be adopted into our coinage system in order to illustrate the wildness of the Senator's language. It was simply this: The Spanish dollar, averaging, as found in circulation here, about 371¼ grains of pure metal, was the coin in which all contracts were made in America. Previous to 1728 the Spanish dollar contained, according to law, 389.4 grains of fine silver, with a remedy of 2 to 3 grains per dollar, the actual range of newly minted coins being 386¼ to 387¼ grains fine. Those weighed by Newton in 1717 yielded 386¾ grains fine. In 1728 the Spanish dollar was reduced by the law of Spain to 383.2 grains fine. In 1772 it was reduced to 374¼ grains fine, with a remedy of 1 grain.

In 1786 the Congress of the American Confederation adopted the dollar as a unit of money of account and fixed its value at 375.64 grains fine; but no actual dollars were coined and none used except Spanish dollars.

In 1792 the Congress of the United States adopted and coined a silver dollar of 371¼ grains fine, and this dollar remained unchanged until to-day, or, practically, until its coinage was forbidden by its omission from the revised mint code of 1873. It, however, remained as it had always been an unlimited legal tender until 1874, when this attribute was destroyed by its erroneous inclusion, among subsidiary silver coins limited to a five-dollar legal tender, in the Revised Statutes. The weight of this dollar was derived from a number of the Spanish dollars in circulation in 1792. The average of these as assayed by Alexander Hamilton was found to be 371 grains, to which Hamilton added one-fourth of a grain to make sure of its being of full average weight. The gold dollar of account was made exactly one-fifteenth of this weight. As Spanish silver dollars were the only money in the United States at the time of the passage of this act, and it was desirable to retain them in circulation for some time after, (they were in fact so retained until 1853,) it was necessary to weight the American silver dollar exactly even with the Spanish dollars in circulation. Had the American silver dollar been made of full weight with newly coined Spanish silver dollars, to wit, 374⅝ grains pure, they would have been melted up and Spanish dollars, slightly abraded, would have usurped their place. Had they been made of less weight than the circulating Spanish dollar the latter would have been driven out of the country, a catastrophe which at that time we could not afford to sustain. They were therefore made to conform to the actual dollar in circulation, the dollar in which all contracts had been made. It was the dollar of Charles V; it was the dollar of the Conquest; it was the dollar of the early colonial establishments; it was the dollar of the Revolution; it was the dollar of the Confederation; it became the dollar of the Union, and it is the dollar of to-day's Centennial, except that by the act of 1873 no new coins of this denomination can be manufactured at the mint and that, through an outrageous blunder of the revisers of the statutes in 1874, it cannot be legally tendered for more than $5. It is these two pernicious restrictions upon the use of the silver dollar that we are attempting to remove; and yet this is the dollar which the Senator stigmatizes as "degraded," and this the attempt which he characterizes as "revolutionary." It is difficult to imagine a more violent misapplication of terms.

What is there about 371¼ grains of pure silver which is "degraded?" What is there degraded or degrading in the employment of this quantity of metal to discharge a debt of one dollar, or a million times this quantity to discharge a debt of a million dollars, if it equitably and fairly measures the debt due? What is there revolutionary in restoring to our laws provisions of which they were deprived by indirection and without public discussion? Is it believed that, were these provisions of law restored, a man who owed, for example, a thousand dollars in greenbacks, would get the better of his creditor by offering to pay him with a thousand silver dollars or a Government certificate of deposit for that amount? Is it supposed that any creditor would object to being paid in silver dollars instead of currency dollars a debt contracted on the currency basis? Of course he would not; for the one is to-day the equivalent of the other. The Senator urges a country now groaning under a heavy burden of debt (aside from the national debt) which is counted in dollars, to choose the scarcest and most costly dollar, a dollar which would give the creditor 15 per cent. more than his just due and punish the debtor in the same proportion, instead of the cheaper silver dollar, which would to-day accurately measure and serve as the equivalent of each dollar of indebtedness in this land. What have the debtors of this country been guilty of, that all the inconveniences and burdens of a return to specie payments should be imposed on them alone?

The fallacy of assuming that the present recent and temporary market ratio between the metals of nearly 18 instead of the long-time relation of 15¼ would continue after the return of this country to specie payments, is to be found not only in the speech of the Senator from Vermont; it vitiates the arguments of all those who, directly or indirectly, have advocated the single gold standard. They all admit that the demonetization of one hundred or two hundred million ounces of silver and their substitution by an equivalent of gold in Germany has chiefly, if not entirely, caused the recent rise in gold from 15¼ to 18 of silver. But at the same time they wholly fail to perceive that the adoption by the United States of the bimetallic standard at such a ratio as will for a time insure the employment of silver to the substantial exclusion of gold would have the tendency, if not the effect, to cause gold to fall again to its normal ratio of 15¼.

That such would be the case, it is impossible to doubt. We have not only the experience of the recent rise in gold upon which to base this expectation; we have also many other similar experiences, and notably the one occasioned by the adoption of the single gold standard by England in 1816, and her purchase of gold for the purpose of resuming specie payments in 1821.

These purchases caused gold to rise in the markets of the world in the course of a few years from its normal ratio of 15¼ to that of 16. Instead of waiting for this abnormal and temporary rise to subside, as it would inevitably have done—for 15¼ and not 16 is the relative cost of the production of gold to silver—our legislators of 1834 changed the legal ratio of the metals to 16. They did this not by increasing the weight of the silver dollar—that has never been changed during the entire history of our country—but by diminishing the weight of the gold one.

Whether this legislation was accomplished in consequence of looking at the question—as I fear some of us are now disposed to do—too narrowly, or because it was supposed that the British demand for gold would continue indefinitely, it is not necessary at this time to inquire. The point is now to ascertain what effect this undervaluation of silver had upon the markets of the world. The effect was not great, for our population then composed but a small part of the civilized world, and the undervaluation was so moderate that our silver stock was melted up quite gradually. But, though small, the effect was the same as in all similar cases. This was a temporary fall in the rejected metal and a temporary rise in the preferred one.

CAUSES OF THE REVULSION OF 1837.

Although the effect upon the world generally was but small, upon this country alone it was considerable. The loss of this silver was one, and not the least, of those causes to which can be traced the financial troubles of that period. Gold was and is too valuable a metal to be coined into pieces smaller than half or quarter eagles, therefore the adoption of a ratio at which silver was undervalued was tantamount to a premium on the issue of small and fractional bank-notes. Such was the importance of obtaining small monetary units that people no longer looked carefully to the resources of the individuals and banks which furnished them, and the wild-cat system flourished throughout the land. In England the emission of small notes is put down with a strong hand, but there never was, and probably will never be, a hand strong enough to put it down in this country. Hence in 1834 commenced that vast issue of notes by private banks, whose united power soon became so great that they attempted to monopolize the entire circulation of the country, and with that view conspired to overthrow the National Bank, and in this they succeeded. Upon the removal of this last restraint upon the recklessness of their operations their emissions were rapidly increased, until from ninety millions in 1834 they rose to one hundred and forty-nine millions in 1837. The country was flooded with irredeemable paper and involved in the wildest speculations. Its stock of silver having been banished through undervaluation, and the meager stock of gold which had come in to take its place being insufficient to keep intact the banks of that mighty channel through which the circulation swept, the stream overflowed and submerged the country in universal bankruptcy.

The effects of the tremendous convulsion of 1837 were felt in a marked degree until the fortunate discovery of gold in California relieved the dearth of metal, and are not entirely effaced even at this distant day. That in no small degree this convulsion had its origin in that mistaken legislation which undervalued and banished silver from the country, there can be no doubt whatever.

ERRONEOUS POLICY.

And yet if we pass the bill before us without an amendment restoring the silver dollar as an unlimited legal tender at about 16 to 1 and with free coinage at cost of manufacture, our legislation will be as mistaken as, nay, far more mistaken than, that of 1834. We shall commit a similar error if we pass the amendment proposed by my friend from Vermont, namely, one requiring the silver dollar to consist of 467.8 grains of standard or 421 grains of pure silver. This would be at the rate of more than 18 of silver for 1 of gold. A silver dollar so heavy and valuable as this would not circulate even now, and the Senator from Vermont well knows it. It would go into the melting-pot. Much less will it circulate when, as an experience of nearly three hundred years fully assures us, gold shall have subsided to its normal market relations to silver.

The object of the Senator's proposed amendment is, therefore, to force the resumption of specie payment in gold dollars and to defeat the effort now being made to resume in silver.

I trust that the Senate will vote down the amendment, or any other which proposes to put more than sixteen times the weight of metal in a silver dollar than into a gold one. As for the proposition to make silver bullion a legal tender at its market value in gold, which is embodied in a bill now before the Senate, I trust that it will be voted down also. It will afford no relief whatever to the country. You might as well make wheat or certificates of deposit therefor a legal tender at its market price in gold. It needs no legislation to effect this object. Every commodity is already, in effect, a legal tender at its market price. It is the increasing dearth of gold which renders these market prices so low as to endanger the solvency of the country; an evil which it is desirable to mitigate. This can only be done by restoring silver to the currency at such a ratio to gold as will enable us to temporarily and partially dispense with the latter. As to this ratio, it is my opinion, and in this I am supported in various communications which I have received from distinguished bimetallists in France and England, that even 16 to 1 is too high. The ratio should be 15¼ to 1. But I am an advocate of the silver dollar as it stood previous to its late almost magical disappearance from our statute-books. I advocate it not so much because it is the dollar in which we have the option of paying our bonded debt, as because it is the dollar with which the obligations, contracts, and debts between the citizens of this country, amounting to thousands of millions of dollars, can be accurately adjusted and equitably settled.

RESUMPTION IN GOLD IMPOSSIBLE.

The Senator from Vermont argues that we shall be just as able to resume payments in gold in 1879 as we were in 1843, when, as he says, "we had less gold than in 1837." In this conclusion I am happy to be able to agree with him, though perhaps not precisely in the same sense. I believe that if it ever takes place at all, the resumption of payments in gold dollars of the present weight will take place in precisely the same way as it did in 1843. We first repudiated nearly all the debts we owed, and then resumed in gold, even, as the Senator says, "with less gold than we had in 1837."

This honorable achievement, which has left a stain upon the escutcheons of some of the foremost States of this Union, would in my opinion be repeated, would have to be repeated, were we to attempt to resume specie payments in gold dollars of the present weight. There are already in existence in several States of this Union organized parties who openly advocate stay-laws for private debts and open repudiation for public ones, and dangerous heresies involving further issues of paper money are gaining ground all over the land.

The Senator has placed the ladder of resumption in an elevator. He would set the country to work toiling and sweating up its rounds in the vain hope of reaching the parlor floor, which is carpeted with gold. The case is more hopeless than that of Sisyphus, whose arid hill-side was at least stationary. But my friend's elevator has the peculiar property of descending the moment anybody attempts to climb his ladder, and of descending faster than the climber can climb. The inevitable result must be that the toiler will soon find himself below the level of solvency and will land in the basement of bankruptcy.

EXTRAVAGANT OBJECTIONS.

Addressing himself more immediately to the provisions of the pending bill, the Senator argues that if the Government does not limit its emissions of the silver for which the bill provides and which it limits to a tender of $20, the Government may redeem with it such a quantity of greenbacks that the emission of silver may be "illimitable" and the country may be "flooded" with it; a result which the Senator appears to regard with great apprehension.

Now, it does not seem clear to me that if there are but three hundred and fifty millions of greenbacks afloat the emission of silver coins to redeem them can be "illimitable," seeing that even three hundred and fifty millions is a limited and not an illimitable sum. Nor does it seem clear to me how the country can be "flooded" with these silver tokens if the paper tokens which they are to replace do not flood the country now; nor if, as the Senator avers, the silver bullion for these tokens can now be bought for even dollars in greenbacks, can I understand how the country can lose anything by afterward redeeming the greenbacks with the silver tokens.

The Senator denies that there are any of our former silver dollars now in circulation; but in this, as I am informed, he is hardly correct. It has been stated that there are some $20,000 in silver dollars now in the Treasury, and I am credibly advised that there are plenty of them doing duty at Philadelphia, Louisville, and elsewhere, in the payment of ground-rents, certain of which the courts have very properly decided can only be discharged in these coins. In addition, there are said to be considerable numbers circulating in South America, China, &c. It is true that the whole amount in circulation in this country is comparatively small; but what of it? Are there any gold dollars in circulation? We all know that, with the exception of a few which are paid into the custom-houses, these little coins are so scarce as to have become almost obsolete. Does not this fact furnish as strong ground for an argument to degrade or interdict the gold dollar as the other does to degrade or interdict the silver dollar?

The Senator alludes at some length to the public debt, the "dishonesty" of proposing to pay it in silver dollars, the danger of inviting it home "in ship loads to be sold for whatever it would bring"—as though it was ever sold for any more—the peril of our not being able to fund it at a lower rate of interest, and so forth. All of this I pass over, because if our public debt is not now and has not always been payable in silver dollars of 371¼ grains pure, then the amendment which I support does not apply to the subject.

The Senator quotes from the British mint report of 1871 to prove that the "chairman of the Committee on Finance [Mr. SHERMAN] was mistaken if he intended to claim that an unlimited double standard existed in England." England abolished the double standard sixty years ago, and the world has never ceased to be reminded of the fact by the continual perturbations in monetary affairs which it occasions.

Passing over the Senator's account of the latest of these perturbations, namely, the recent coinage movements and regulations in Germany, and the Latin union, I come upon this statement in his speech:

Since 1870 the price [of silver] in London, the great market for silver, has varied from 60*d.* per ounce to 52*d.*, or nearly 16 per cent., which is actually more than the variation, during the same period, of our paper money.

The pence in which the Senator's quotations are expressed are standard gold. Now, suppose that instead of quoting the price of silver in standard gold, he had quoted the price of gold in standard silver, let us see how the paragraph would read :

"Since 1870 the price [of gold] in London, the great market for gold, has varied nearly 16 per cent., which is infinitely more than the variation, during the same period, of our paper money," which in silver, during the period mentioned, has scarcely varied at all.

To quote the prices of gold in silver for the purpose of showing a variation in the relative value of the two metals is as correct and fair as to quote the prices of silver in gold. Neither of them is correct. The only way to ascertain which metal has altered is to measure them in some third commodity. If this be done, it will be found that silver has not fallen at all; but that, on the contrary, gold has risen. By the other method, which is not argument at all but a mere trick of quotations, one is led to suppose that gold is absolutely immovable, while all other commodities, silver included, are subject to the most violent fluctuations. By the true method, which *is* argument, it will be found that all commodities fluctuate in value; but silver among the least of all.

ENORMOUS ESTIMATES OF FUTURE SUPPLY OF SILVER.

As to the Senator's estimates of the future silver product of the United States and Mexico, I can only say that I have not been able to find support for them either in books, official reports, or from my own private information. They appear to me loose, excessive, and misleading. They ignore the fact that while the product has increased in this country, it has fallen off in others; that while it has increased in some mines, it has fallen off in others; and that the successful exploration of the Bonanza mines has been concurrent with the abandonment and closure of numerous others which previously yielded a large amount of silver. This fact the Senator himself inferentially admits in another part of his speech.

Yet to strengthen his excessive estimates of this product the Senator claims that "notwithstanding the recent enormous yields of the gold-fields of California and Australia" silver has fallen in ratio to gold from 15.7 in 1849 to 18.13 at the present time. My reply to this statement is that there has been no "recent enormous yield of gold." On the contrary, the annual gold product of the world has fallen off from over one hundred and ninety millions in 1852 to scarcely one-half this sum in 1875; and it is to other causes than the vicissitudes of mining that we must look for the recent change it the long-standing ratio between the metals.

SILVER CONSUMED IN THE ARTS.

I must also demur to the Senator's sweeping implication that less silver is used in the arts now than formerly, or, as he puts it, when "barbaric displays" were wont to be made of silver dishes.

In his testimony before the British parliamentary committee now sitting in England, on this very subject, Mr. Ernest Seyd, a technically qualified authority on the subject, estimated the annual consumption of silver in the arts at 2,000,000 ounces in England alone, at or about two and a half million ounces in France, at somewhat under 2,000,000 ounces in Germany, and at some 10,000,000 ounces for all Europe. Add to these an allowance for North, South, and Central Americas, in all of which portions of the world, silver, in proportion to population, is more commonly employed in the arts than in Europe, and an allowance for Asia, Africa, and Australia, and the estimate would approximate the figures of Wolowski and other authorities on the subject, who reckon the consumption in the arts throughout the world at one-half the entire product, or about 36,000,000 ounces.

If the days of "barbaric displays" of silver dishes carry us back to the year 1829, they occurred during a period when the entire silver product of the world was, according to McCulloch, less than one-half the amount, which, as above shown, is now used up in the arts alone. Indeed, the consumption of silver in the arts at the present time nearly equals the whole product of the world at so late a date as 1861, when, according to the Journal des Économistes, the entire silver product of the world was but $42,500,000 per annum.

In the face of these facts I am at a loss to understand upon what authority or information the Senator relies for his inference that the consumption of silver in the arts has fallen off.

Recurring to the production of silver he avers that "the Consolidated Virginia mine produces $3,600,000 of silver and gold in one month, at a cost, as reported, of only $300,000," and argues that "other mines of silver must close up or the price of silver must fall."

The idea which the Senator seems to convey in this passage—though he really does not say so—is that the Consolidated Virginia is a great silver mine which produces 12 of result for 1 of investment, and that consequently the price of silver must fall.

In the first place, it does not follow that, because a particular mine yields $12 for $1 in current expenses, the market value of its product will fall. In such a calculation the capital invested, the capital sunk in other similar enterprises where the product failed entirely, the demand for consumption, and many other elements, are necessary factors. The price is the average cost of producing silver everywhere.

Such prizes as the Consolidated Virginia Company has been fortunate enough to find, have lured on to their ruin thousands of mining companies, which, after expending years of effort and millions of capital in a vain search for similar deposits, have been obliged to abandon their enterprises; and this is continually going on and forms a part of the history of mining. It is through explorations of this character that, at rare intervals, a bonanza is discovered. Hence the capital sunk in unsuccessful prospecting adventures must be considered as much a part of the cost of the production of the precious metals, as the capital which represents the current expenses of a successful mine.

The Senator's statement that the yield of the Consolidated Virginia mine for a single month was $3,600,000 and the cost of production $300,000 would inferentially lead to the belief that this great yield was almost, if not entirely, of silver. True, he refers to the yield as one of gold and silver, but he slurs over the word gold and dwells with emphasis upon the word silver. He evidently cites this example to prove that a commodity whose cost of production is but 10 per cent. of its market price must rapidly decline in value, until market price and cost price closely approximate each other. If the yield were entirely of silver, the argument would be narrow which drew the facts to support it from the history of the operations of a single mine in a single month. But what sort of a point is it that he makes against the stability of value in silver, in the presence of the fact that nearly half of this great yield was of gold, produced, of course, with as little cost as was the silver. His argument commences with being specious and ends with being illogical. It either proves nothing, or it proves too much.

EMPTY ASSERTIONS.

The Senator's speech contains a great number of statements and deductions which he has not fortified with proper authority. I shall therefore simply repeat a few of them, rapidly commenting on each as it comes under review. He says:

European nations shaking off their heavy loads of silver coin. * * * A diminishing market in India; diminishing ever since it was gorged by the influx of silver arising from the cotton famine in England.

This measure—the bill before the Senate—would also be a great wrong upon the laboring-men of the country. They are impatiently waiting for a return to specie payments.

Being 10 or 12 per cent. below gold the laborer would suffer—by being paid in silver—to that extent. If he still owed a mortgage on his house or farm it would have to be paid in gold, but his $20 of wages would be paid in silver. * * * The evils of inflation would remain in full force and to the same extent. * * * By starting a legal tender of silver dollars at 10 or 12 per cent. below the standard of gold, gold must either be debased or be hustled out of the country. The survival not of the fittest but of the poorest only is possible under the laws of trade.

Silver may answer for the currency of countries having little home trade and less foreign commerce, but will not answer for the large trade of enterprising peoples, nor of nations competing for high positions in all the markets of the world. Silver is insufficient and inappropriate for the American people or for the United States.

These extracts are all from the Senator's speech. They can be answered in a few words. If European nations are shaking off their heavy loads of silver, they are also shaking off prosperity with it, and will eventually have to buy it back, but can never do so at the price they are selling it for. In fact, there is not nearly enough silver in Europe to redeem the inconvertible paper afloat. Nor is India gorged with it, for labor commands there but a few pence per day. A small rise in general prices in that country, which is inevitable, will absorb all the surplus silver. As soon as this is accomplished India bills will again command a premium in gold in London.

The laboring-man instead of losing will profit by a resumption in silver, in that he would receive a stable value-money instead of credit-money for his services. The value of his labor and the silver dollar would readily adjust themselves to each other. He could pay the mortgage on his house in silver dollars, which would accurately and equitably measure the value of the dollar the mortgage called for; but in case of resumption in gold, his labor and everything else but the mortgage on his house would shrink in value; it would become too heavy for him to raise, and would have to be canceled by a sheriff's deed.

ASSUMED OSCILLATION OF THE METALS.

Says the Senator:

With a double standard we should have a double lack of uniformity, with oscillations hither and thither, and ever fitfully sinking to the lowest point of either one or the other of the competing metals.

With a double standard there would be no oscillations tending downward; and instead of a double lack of uniformity, there would be a double security for stability. For it is to be borne in mind and is a fact of vital consequence to this discussion, a fact which seems to have been overlooked by all writers on this subject, that the oscillations in the price of the two metals, their change in relative value, is not occasioned by a decline in the one metal, but by an advance in the other. This advance is of a spasmodic character, and is caused, not by the inadequate current production of the advancing metal—for any change from this cause is of slow growth—but by the sudden demand of some particular country in times of overtrading, speculation, and panic; some country which exclusively uses such metal as money. It was this kind of a demand which in this country in the panic of 1873 caused greenbacks to command a premium over bank-notes, and, notwithstanding that the business outlook was never more gloomy, caused them to approximate more nearly to a parity with gold than they had done for years in the most prosperous times. When one of her periodical panics sweeps over England, gold goes to a premium over silver, which in such crisis is of no use to her. So in Austria, when she is overtaken by a financial storm, silver is in great demand and commands a premium over gold, because silver is Austria's sole debt-paying commodity. In neither case does the other metal decline in value, but bears the same relation to general commodities as before.

The countries wise enough to base their financial systems on the double standard always retain the stationary metal, the metal which accurately and equitably measures the obligations between men by an exchange for it of the other and temporary dearer metal at a profit to themselves. The history of monetary panics shows that such panics are more severe and of much longer duration in single and especially gold standard countries than in countries of the double standard. The reason for this is apparent. In the one case only one-half of the world's stock of precious metals can be drawn on for relief; and in the other case, the whole. The only exception that can arise to this rule governing the change of the relations of the metals, is, when a country unwisely demonetizes one of the metals and sells it for less than its cost to them or its cost of production. This is what Germany is now attempting to do; and therefore gold has temporarily risen in the same proportion that silver has fallen. Such a derangement in the relation of the metals can .only be temporary. The cost of production must govern the relation; and when changes in the standard of countries have ceased to operate by reason of the absorption of their surplus stock by other countries, or its consumption in the arts, the old-time relation must of necessity be restored. Under such circumstances it is profitable for other countries to adopt the discarded metal, for it is then cheaper than it can be produced or than it is likely to be again.

THE OPTIONAL STANDARD.

The Senator says:

It has been argued that a double standard of gold and silver will prevent oscillations.

The Senator will, I trust, pardon me if I doubt that such an argument has ever been made. The argument is not that the double standard will prevent oscillations, but that, like the combination of two different metals in the balance-wheel of a watch, it will lessen them. Far more important than this, however, is the merit it possesses of utilizing as money the entire stock of coin in the world, which even then is so inadequate to the requirements of industry that it has to be eked out with every form, safe and unsafe, of negotiable paper, in order that exchanges may be made and such prices maintained as will permit an equitable settlement between debtor and creditor.

HISTORY OF THE AMERICAN DOLLAR.

The Senator avers that Hamilton made a mistake of fact in putting but 371¼ grains of pure silver in the dollar instead of 377¼ grains. If the Senator will consult our official documents upon this subject he will find that Hamilton made no mistake at all. His very proper object, as he himself expressed it, was to coin a dollar of the same weight of pure silver as the Spanish dollar then circulating in this country, because it was in this dollar that all our contracts had been made. To ascertain this weight, as I have before stated, he caused a number of Spanish dollars, then current, to be assayed, and found them to contain on the average about 371¼ grains pure. It was for this reason that he recommended the American dollar to be coined of this weight. Had he put any more silver into it he would have committed precisely the same error which the distinguished Senator from Vermont now advises. The country was in debt then as it is now. Hamilton desired that this debt should be paid to the full and honorably. To accomplish this purpose he did not deem it necessary to pay it in dollars containing each of them any more silver than could be purchased by the current dollar of the day. He thought it sufficient if the new dollar contained exactly as much metal as the current dollar could purchase; and this was the course pursued. And mark the result. Instead of earning for the country the violent reproaches of dishonor, repudiation, violation of contracts, &c., which the Senator would heap upon a similar measure at the present time, it strengthened its credit and gave it a high place among borrowing nations.

THE AMERICAN MINES AND AMERICAN DOLLAR.

The Senator next alludes to the fact that the American gold eagle, which was established in 1792 at 270 grains standard, was reduced in

1834 to 258 grains standard; he avers that the change was made chiefly to obviate the rise or fall of one or the other of the precious metals, and he concludes that therefore—

A double legal-tender standard of coins cannot circulate together and be interchangeable unless at the time of equal intrinsic value, except in the case of limited coinage of small denominations required for change.

The whole of this argument is confused and illogical. When any portion of a coinage is limited, the system of coinage cannot be one of a double standard. The double standard involves a fixed relation between silver and gold, both of which may be coined illimitably and of any denominations required by those who present the bullion at the mints. If the market value and the legal relation coincide, there will be no advantage in tendering coins of one metal for debt over coins of the other. In case they do not coincide the debtor will, of course, choose coins of the cheaper metal in paying, as he had to receive the cheaper when he borrowed. This is the option which, up to 1816, or rather 1821, existed in all the countries of the Western world, and up to within the last few years in all those countries except England, and that Mr. Dupont-White held in view when he exclaimed that Columbus had brought from across the Atlantic the means of liberating the masses of Europe from the thralldom of feudalism. It is not claimed that an exact coincidence between the legal and market relations of the metals can always be maintained; but it is claimed that if the legal relation be fixed at an average, covering a long period of years, the closest approximation to equity between debtor and creditor will be attained. First one and then the other metal will be used; now in one and then in the other country; and the prices of commodities and services will be measured, not by the total of one stock, but by the total of both stocks of metals.

The universal adoption of the single gold standard, which by precept and example you are advocating, would cause such a depreciation in the prices of commodities and services as would break up all the relations of society, bankrupt nations, and impoverish debtors throughout the world.

Recurring now to the Senator's allusion to the reduction of the gold eagle in 1834, does this fact not furnish the strongest evidence that it was and has been and is the silver dollar which is the measure of debt in this country, and not the gold dollar or any other dollar? We adopted the current Spanish dollar in 1792 because that was the dollar in which debts had been incurred; we stuck to the same dollar in 1834, when the market relation between silver and gold had been changed by the blundering and mischievous legislation of England and the vicissitudes of supply and demand; and we stuck to it even after the opening of California, when the gold dollar became cheaper than the silver one; because the history of the world assured us that gold would fluctuate again, and the gold dollar would rise above the silver one. We never surrendered the option of tendering whichever of the two dollars we chose. It was while the option existed that we went into the late war and that we got into debt to each other and to foreigners. The promise to pay so many dollars, which is printed on our national notes and our bank-notes and our State, municipal, and corporative bonds, either meant or means so many dollars, either of 371¼ grains of pure silver or 23.22 grains of pure gold, at the option and pleasure of the debtor; or else it has no reference to metal at all and means so many "dollars". in paper promises. The attempt which has been made to convert these promises, which amount in the aggregate to several thousand millions, into promises to pay gold dollars, by means of the mint act of 1873 and the revision act of 1874, I declare to be entirely unprecedented and unconstitutional.

COINAGE OF SILVER.

The Senator from Vermont says that "the issue of any large amount of silver-dollar coinage has never been the policy of the United States;" that "from 1793 to 1805, inclusive, the whole amount coined was $1,439,512;" that "from 1805 to 1836 not a dollar was struck at the Mint;" that from "1793 up to and including 1840 the whole amount coined was $1,501,822;" that "since 1840 the whole amount coined has been $6,544,016," and that "the total of the silver dollars struck at all the mints of the United States from 1793 up to this day amounts to no more than $8,045,833," and he adduces a long table from the Mint records to support these statements.

The Senator concludes that—

These facts show the inconsiderable figure that silver dollars have played in our monetary affairs from the foundation of the Government and the groundlessness of the complaint relative to the law of 1873.

With all deference for the opinions of the distinguished Senator, I maintain that they show nothing of the kind. From 1792 up to 1873 the people of this country enjoyed the option of paying their debts in either the silver or the gold dollar at pleasure. Because they may have chosen during the most active portion of this period to pay them in gold dollars in consequence of the fact that gold dollars were cheaper than silver ones is surely no reason why they should without any consideration whatever have been divested of that option by an obscure coinage act of whose purport and tremendous significance they were not avised.

But the Senator did not give us all the facts in this connection. He omitted to state that we were producing no silver in this country during that period and that Spanish silver dollars and fractions of dollars were in circulation in this country to a very large amount and that up to 1853 they were a full legal tender at their talo value for

the payment of debts, and to that extent obviated the necessity and
expense of coinage at our own mints. He also omitted to state that
American half dollars, quarters, dimes, and half dimes, which were
coined in large amounts, were also full-weighted and full legal tenders up to 1853. If he will add to this eight millions of silver dollars
all the Spanish and other foreign silver coins in circulation in this
country and all the silver fractional currency coined at the mints, all
of which were full legal tenders for the payments of debts up to 1853,
he will then and only then be able to furnish us with all the facts in
the case. When he does this it will be found that, instead of playing
an inconsiderable figure in the circulation of this country, legal-
tender silver played the most important figure until the time when
gold was overvalued by the law of 1834.

STOCK OF THE PRECIOUS METALS.

"Silver is urged to the front," continues the Senator, "because it
is now more abundant and consequently cheaper than gold; so is copper; so is iron," &c. I have already shown, and at some length*, the
reasons why copper, iron, and all other metals or substances, except
silver and gold, are incapable of efficiently performing the functions
of money. None of these other substances, except, perhaps, platina,
possesses the requisite characteristics for a measure of value. Even
platina, which possesses every necessary intrinsic quality, is deficient
in a respect which is almost as important as an intrinsic quality;
there is no great stock of it on hand in the world; no reservoir from
the ages to steady the fluctuations in prices, which, if it were used as
money, would be occasioned by the vicissitudes of its current supply
from the mines. This point I illustrated heretofore by adducing the
history of platina coins in Russia, and it is this point especially that
forms the strongest argument in favor of monetizing silver as a legal
tender for the payment of debts to any amount. Let me quote from
the most recent publication on the subject:

The essay on bimetallic money by M. DeLavelye, which the Senator from Ohio [Mr. SHERMAN] called attention to the other day, says:

As is well known, the precious metals have a tolerably stable value, because, the
annual supply forming only one-sixtieth of the whole stock of the world, an
increase or decrease of the annual product is only slightly felt, and would have to
continue constant in order to have much influence. The larger the stock the less
will any increment or decrement in the supply of gold or silver affect the value
of the whole quantity. If you admit into the circulation both gold and silver, the
stock of specie will be about fifty milliards; if you exclude silver it will be only
about twenty-seven or twenty-eight milliards. Being thus reduced it would be
more easily affected by an increase or decrease of the supply. Suppose that after
1850 gold had been demonetized, as was advised by M. Michel Chevalier, what an
enormous fall in value would gold not have sustained; following a sudden increment of half a milliard of annual production. What a rapid rise of prices would
have occurred in countries where gold money was employed! As was set forth by
the Netherlands monetary commission of 1873, the coinage of gold into money in

---

* See speech of April 24, 1876, on "Resumption and the Double Standard."

countries where the double standard is employed served as a parachute to prevent the degradation of that metal and the mischief which would have resulted from it.

And yet the very class of men whose interests were thus saved from annihilation by the double standard, the creditor class, the fund-holders, mortgagees, and annuitants, are those who would abolish the double standard and limit silver to the base office of fractional token money. Nothing but the narrowest selfishness or short-sightedness could possibly urge men to commit a blunder which, in case of the discovery of new and extensive gold placers, might greatly endanger the very interests which they would now so unjustly and unwisely enhance. Such a contingency is by no means remote. The entire continent of Africa is being laid open to the explorer, and that vast portion of the earth would have to differ from all the other great divisions of the globe if it should fail to yield what they have each yielded in turn, vast alluvial deposits of gold, washed out of the rocks by the rains of centuries.

THE CRESCENDO AND DIMINUENDO THEORY OF MONEY.

I shall conclude my reply to the speech of the Senator from Vermont with noticing the parting shot, the Parthian arrow, which he discharges at some of my previous remarks.

The Senator is sarcastic over the supposed connection between the movement of the currency and incendiary fires, marriages, divorces, homicides, suicides, and other crimes, and asks if I regard silver as the great panacea for these evils. I never referred particularly to silver in this connection. My argument was that while the volume of any currency was diminishing, whether that currency was of silver or gold or paper or anything else, or all combined, prices would fall, the normal relation of debts, commodities, and services would become deranged, and that this would aggravate the various social disorders noticed.

To support this view I will briefly quote from three authors of repute, namely, G. R. Porter, esq., the economist, Henry Thomas Buckle, the historian, and Dr. William Farr, the registrar-general of England:

It is curious to observe how intimate a relation exists between the price of food (and price, of course, depends upon currency) and the number of marriages. * * * The relation that subsists between the price of food and the number of marriages is not confined to our own country; and it is not improbable that, had we the means of ascertaining the facts, we should see the like result in every civilized community. We possess the necessary returns from France, and these fully bear out the view that has been given.—*Porter's Progress of the Nation*, volume 2, pages 244, 245; London, 1838.

It is now known that marriages bear a fixed and definite relation to the price of corn; and in England the experience of a century has proved that * * * they (marriages) are simply regulated by the average earnings of the great mass of the people; so that this immense social and religious institution is not only swayed but is completely controlled by the price of food and the rate of wages.—*Buckle's History of Civilization*, volume 1, page 24, Appleton's edition.

The marriages of 1830 and 1831 exhibit the excess which since 1750 has been invariably observed when the substantial earnings of the people are above the average.—*Dr. Farr in the London Statistical Journal for June,* 1852, page 185.

If the Senator demands that a direct connection shall be established between the prices of wheat in all Europe and the annual supplies of gold and silver in all the world, he will find it fully set forth for a period covering one hundred and twenty-six years, in a work on currency by Joseph Heath, London, 1841, page 81.

REPLY TO SENATOR SHERMAN.

The speech of the distinguished chairman of the Finance Committee [Mr. SHERMAN] is very unlike that of the Senator from Vermont.

It seeks to defeat the restoration of the double standard, not by direct antagonism, but in disarming its advocates by going a portion of the way with them and promising to go further when they shall have surrendered.

The Senator admits the supernal importance of silver in the money of the world and the necessity of restoring it to our coinage, and therefore of the weight and consequence of the amendments which I have had the honor to propose. He admits the legality of the double standard, for he refers to the silver dollar as a "legal tender until 1873, and in strict law" (the Senator would surely have no loose law in the important matter of contracts) "might be restored to the position it then occupied as a standard of value without a violation of the legal contracts between the United States and the bondholders;" and "if a contract made before 1873 was stipulated to be paid in coin, it could undoubtedly be paid in silver as well as gold coin, and those contracts payable in coin can be and ought to be payable in the coin made a legal tender when the contract was made or was payable, and ought not to be affected by a subsequent law." He admits the honesty and respectability of the silver dollar proposed in the bill, for he calls it "the old time-honored standard of silver dollars of full weight and fineness." He admits the value of the silver dollar, for he calls it "the real dollar that pays where it goes," and distinguishes it from "a paper dollar, which only promises to pay." He admits that the present extraordinary rise in gold, or as I think he erroneously states it, the silver "depreciation, grows mainly, if not exclusively, from the action of foreign governments in dealing with their coin," and therefore impliedly admits that the restoration of silver to its long-time place in the money of this country would tend to counteract the assumed depreciation by increasing the demand for silver and diminishing the demand for gold.

All these things he admits, for I have quoted his opinions in his own language; yet, most strange to say, in almost the same breath he seems to deny them all. He denies the importance of silver in the money of the world, except for the purpose of a degraded token coinage; "for," says he, "the bimetallic system, with all its uncertainties at a time when it has been rejected or is being rejected by all commercial nations," and "the objections to the bimetallic system is that, from the nature of things, it is impossible to fix the true relation of silver and gold to each other, and when either advances in value a single hair it becomes demonetized and flees the country." And, concludes the Senator on this head, "they" (the advocates of the pending amendments to restore the double standard) "raise the most difficult questions of political economy and the most delicate questions affecting the public credit, and at a time when above all others we ought not to attempt to decide them." He denies the legality of the double standard, "for," says he, "all contracts payable in coin prior to 1873 were impliedly payable in gold coin," and "ever since 1853 silver coin has been practically a legal tender only for $5;" and "why disturb this *law?*"

Again he says: "This policy," the single gold standard, or, as he styles it, "the composite standard, was adopted by Great Britain in 1815 and by the United States in 1853;" and "it is far wiser for us to stand by the composite standard in force in the United States since 1853;" and "such is the basis of the report of the Committee on Finance." Again, while he is in favor of recoining the old silver dollar, he would limit its use by denying it legal-tender functions for sums over $20 and by restricting its free coinage. Evidently he desires to make these coins pass current for more than their bullion value, and thus make all the retail every-day business of the country rest on a false basis. Such conditions as these should have no place in any sound monetary system.

The criticisms I shall make on the propositions advanced by the honorable Senator will be very brief. The bill as it stands proposes to limit the silver dollar in the payment of debts to sums of not more than $20 in any one payment. The amendment proposes to restore the silver dollar to its constitutional, proper, long-time, place in the monetary system of the country: that of an unlimited legal tender.

This is not raising a difficult or delicate question; it is not, as the Senator elsewhere calls it, an "inopportune consideration," or "a radical change in the existing law," or the "expression of extreme opinions." On the contrary, when stripped of the sophistries by which its opponents endeavor to obscure it, it is a perfectly simple question. There is no better time to decide it than the present. It proposes no radical change in the law, but simply restores the law as it existed from 1792 to 1873, when it was changed without consultation with the people, who were so deeply interested in its provisions.

SOPHISMS.

The Senator avers that the bill without the amendments "prepares the way for resumption in gold by laying a foundation of silver coin," and in another place assures us that it will give us all the silver that will circulate at par with gold. To these somewhat confident assurances I respectfully demur. I deny that the prosperity of the country would be enhanced by a speedy resumption in gold. I believe that there are insuperable difficulties in the way of such resumption. I do not believe that token silver will bring us any nearer resumption than token paper. Gold resumption, as at present advocated, means that the payment of all currency debts, public and private, shall be in dollars, each containing 25.8 grains of standard gold. No amount of silver coinage, bound down by legal-tender limits to petty transactions, would materially assist the people to resume on these rigorous terms; but restore the old silver dollar, unhampered and unrestricted, as it was from 1792 to 1873, and you will furnish the people with a real dollar, worth almost exactly the same as the paper dollar, and one which would equitably settle obligations and contracts without injustice to debtor or creditor. By its increased use it would slowly but surely appreciate to its old-time relation with gold; and thus in safety, and without shock or disturbance, you would reach that very resumption in gold which you desire, and reach it over a solid highway of silver.

Anything short of an unlimited legal tender and free and unrestricted coinage for silver will prove a delusion and a snare.

THE PUBLIC CREDITOR.

The Senator holds that "the serious effects of such a proposition upon our national character and credit cannot be measured in dollars and cents," and in this I agree with him; only I go further, I do not believe that it can be measured in anything whatever, simply because it can have no effect, certainly no disastrous effect, upon that character or credit.

Rather would it degrade that character and injure that credit were we to permit our creditors, and at their pleasure, to violate their contracts with us by refusing to accept silver dollars when by the terms of the contracts they had agreed at our option to receive silver or gold. They would inevitably come to suppose that, by ringing the changes on "honor" and "dishonor," they could do anything they pleased with us and alter our monetary system and the terms of contracts at will.

What is it they ask for? Do they appeal to the equities of the case? Then let us open up the original transactions and see what they gave us for our bonds. I think it will be found that for each dollar of them they paid us about sixty cents in the then cheaper metal or its equivalent; and equity would pay them but sixty cents in the now cheaper metal or its equivalent in return. Do they appeal to the law of the case? The law makes the bonds payable in coin at the rate of 25.8 grains of standard gold or 412.5 grains of standard silver, at the option of the Government. The option was theirs then when they loaned ; the option is ours now when we pay.

When an agent of the Government offers to sell its bonds upon the market, what questions are asked by those to whom they are offered ?

"Is the agent authorized ?

"Are the bonds genuine ?

"When and where are they payable, and with what options or conditions of time and place ?

"In what money or option of moneys are the principal and interest payable ?

"What is the rate of interest, and at what intervals of time, at what places, and with what option of moneys or other conditions, is the interest payable ? "

Where are the answers to these questions found ? Are they sought for in common rumor or the word of the agent ? Nothing of the sort. The lenders find them in the law, and this determines the price they are willing to offer for the bonds. If there is any ambiguity about the law, the ambiguity is measured and deducted from the price offered for the bond. If the law is clear and reserves certain options or conditions to the borrower, those options or conditions are measured and their estimated value deducted from the price. No man voluntarily shuts his eyes when he is lending money, and of all men who look closely to their own interest you may depend upon the public creditor.

Well, then, what does the law say ? I need scarcely repeat it. It says that a dollar is so much gold or so much silver, at the option of the payor; and the payee must accept it or nothing.

As I have before stated, I do not care to enter into a discussion as to the legality or policy of paying either the interest or principal, or both, of the public debt in silver. It is not important to the argument. If it shall be deemed wise policy under existing circumstances to strengthen our credit by giving a bonus to our creditors, well and good. I deem it an entirely unimportant matter alongside of the question of the justice and policy of paying our other debts, State, municipal, corporative, and individual, in silver. Nobody claims that these other debts are payable in gold. They amount to a sum far transcending that of the national debt.

THE DEBTOR CLASS.

According to a speech delivered at Oshkosh, Wisconsin, October 1, 1874, by Mr. JAMES G. BLAINE, the sum of the debts of our cities amounted at that date to five hundred and seventy millions, of our counties to one hundred and eighty millions, and of our States to three hundred and ninety millions, making a total of eleven hundred and forty millions. To this sum may be added ten thousand millions of individual and corporative debts, making altogether eleven thousand one hundred and forty millions, which, if this bill is passed without the amendments, will have to be paid in gold; whilst if it is passed with the amendments, they may be paid in silver. If these debts are attempted to be paid in gold, this metal, which is now 15 per cent. above silver under the old relation, may, and probably would, rise to 20 or 25 per cent. If paid in silver, gold would probably fall to par in silver at the old-time relation of 16 for 1. This is the overwhelming consideration that must give us pause. These State, municipal, corporative, and individual debts, amounting to five times as much as the national debt, by comparison, sink the latter into insignificance.

MINT FACILITIES.

I cannot pass over the Senator's objection, which, should the silver dollar be deemed a good legal tender for the national debt, would have some application to the amendment proposed. He says that with our present mint facilities we could not have enough of silver dollars coined in three years to pay the interest on the national debt, and therefore warns us against coining any of them. I do not see the force of this logic. If we cannot coin enough silver dollars for the purpose intimated, that is no good reason why we should not coin all we can, nor why we should not pay all we can in that metal, if it be right to pay out any of it for this purpose, and the remainder in gold. He seems to apprehend a scarcity of silver, while the Senator from Vermont fears that there would be a redundancy, or, as he terms it, "a flood of it." They may both be wrong but they certainly cannot both be right, and I leave them to offset each other.

FREE MONEY.

I trust that it will be clearly understood that the advocates of bi-metallic money do not purpose to make either of the precious metals a legal tender for any more than their value in the markets of the world. We propose no debased money; no tokens; no money to pay the creditor which is not as valuable as the money he advanced; no untrue or arbitrary relations between the metals; no scheme of advantage to the owners of gold or silver mines, nor to anybody except the people at large. Our proposition is to coin both gold and silver bullion at cost for all comers and make the coins a legal tender for all amounts. The relation we propose is the old one of 16 for 1. The experience of centuries teaches us to believe that this is approximately the relative cost of production. If this is true, let nations tamper with their coins as they may, it will inevitably become the market relation. If the large additional use be given to silver which the amendments to this bill contemplate, that market relation which has long continued would be speedily re-established. If, on the other hand, the relation is fixed at 16½ or 17, or any figure over 16, all hopes of our being able to utilize our product, or Europe's rejected stock of silver, will be defeated. We should either be driven to the exclusive employment of gold or else new legislation and a new ratio, involving the expense and delay of a recoinage, would have to be established.

Our argument is for free money. We regard all restrictions upon money as pernicious, and that there is as much and no more right on the part of the Government to limit the use of money at its free market value as there is to limit the use of bread, meat, or other commodities whose exchangeable value money is designed to measure.

We hold that the employment of silver and gold in the arts is essential to the retention of their worth as money, and that this employment acts as a parachute to retard and lessen the fluctuations incited by the vicissitudes of their production in the mines; we hold that nothing can be good money which can be used for money alone; we are opposed to token coins or coins to which the law gives a value which the market denies, believing that their use is fraught with peril of insecurity, injustice, panic, and counterfeiting; and we believe that no form of credit can by itself properly serve the purposes of money, and that its use should always be voluntary and never forced.

By money is meant gold and silver coins, with the option of employing either one or the other at a ratio based upon the experience of long periods of time. This option was enjoyed by the people of this country from 1792 to 1873. It was secured to them by the terms of the Constitution, and though attempted to be taken from them by the mint act of 1873 and the Revised Statutes of 1874, the option is theirs yet, and they cannot be deprived of it by legislation.

OPTIONS IN CONTRACTS.

Have Senators well considered the importance of an option in a money contract? The United States Government issues bonds payable at its own option at any time after five years or before twenty years. This is its option. The Government may call in and pay off these bonds after five years, or it may not choose to do so until twenty years. The case is similar with other bonds issued by this Government, the ten-forties, the twenty-forties, &c. This option it paid for by accepting a lower price for the bonds than they would have commanded had the option been omitted. Thus far the Government has not availed itself of its option in any of these last-named bonds and it may never do so. But is this any reason why it may not lawfully and honorably do so if it chooses? And is there any reason, because it did not choose to exercise its option of paying silver dollars up to 1873, why it may not lawfully and honorably do so now?

The whole object of an option as to time, or metal, or any other particular of a contract, between debtor and creditor, is to prevent one party from crowding or cornering the other, or to take advantage of favorable turns in the market.

Unless we reserved a time option in our bonds, they might be presented for payment at an inconvenient moment, when we could not meet them or when the rate of interest for money was unusually high. Unless we reserved an option of metals in which our debts could be discharged, we might be called upon to pay them in a temporarily scarce or cornered metal, such as gold is to-day.

Is the creditor "cheated" when the debtor makes avail of an option which forms an explicit and distinctive feature of his contract? Does the debtor "dishonor" himself by choosing whether he shall pay in five years or twenty, in gold or in silver, at one place or another, provided his contract gives him these options? I should say not. Justice, common sense, plain English say not; but certain Senators here say "Yes." They prophesy an immediate downfall of our credit, "the return of our bonds in ship-loads," says one of them, should we choose to exercise our option, which we paid for, and of the right to which nothing short of an amendment to the Constitution can deprive us.

THE NEW YORK TRIBUNE.

An influential metropolitan journal of recent date says:

Prior to 1873 all debts contracted to be paid in coin were legally and equitably payable in gold or silver.

It is just as immoral to change the obligation of contracts in the interest of the creditor as to change the obligation of contracts in the interest of the debtor.

The unexpected fall in the price of silver or rise in gold in no way affects obligations legally and equitably payable, according to the terms of the contract, either in gold or in silver coin.

The question whether the single or the double standard should be adopted with respect to future transactions should depend solely upon the general public interest, and in no degree upon the private interest of individuals as owners of gold mines or of silver mines, as debtors or creditors.

These propositions are followed by an extended article, in which they are worked out with ability.

The writer, however, falls into one very extraordinary error, and, as it is upon an essential point of the whole subject, I cannot do better than to notice it in this place.

He says that the position of the advocates of the double standard has been weakened by resorting to the argument that to demonetize silver all over the world would practically double all its debts. He contests this upon the ground that "the various forms of credit used as currency affect prices *quite as much* as coin itself, and that an insignificant proportion of modern transactions in civilized countries are settled by payments of money." This insignificant proportion he assumes, for the sake of argument, to be 1 of money to 20 of "credits used as currency." Hence, he concludes that, if the demonetization of silver should result in no "*increased* use of credits, it would lessen by not more than one-fortieth the amount of currency used at the chief commercial centers in determining prices."

Without assenting to either of the propositions that the use of a given sum in credits used as currency, say bank-checks, or even bank-notes, affects prices *quite as much* as a similar sum in money, or that the proportion in use of one to the other is as 20 is to 1, both of which propositions I deny, it is enough if it be agreed on both sides that a vast superstructure of credits rests upon a comparatively small base of real money, and that both money and credits assist to support prices. I say that to take away one-half of the base, as you would do if you demonetized silver, would be tantamount to destroying one-half of the superstructure, and, consequently, to the doubling of all debts, while the critic holds that you may remove one-half of the base without disturbing the superstructure, and consequently without affecting prices or the relation of prices to debts.

As it is essential to this argument to determine which is right, I propose to test both arguments by altering the proportions assumed in the examples. According to my doctrine if you remove one-half *or any other proportion* of the base, you destroy the same proportion of the superstructure, and my correctness is demonstrated very conclusively by the table of prices of wheat referred to in a previous part of this speech. According to the critic, you may remove one-half of the base without affecting the superstructure. If you can remove one-half without perturbation you can remove five-eighths, three-fourths, seven-eighths, or even the whole of it, and prices would remain the same. If the critic is right we need no specie basis at all.

And this is precisely the attitude of those Senators who favor the demonetization of silver or its degradation to the position of a token. A token coinage is a credit coinage, the extent of the credit, which is enforced by law, being exactly that of the difference between the legal and the market value of the metals contained in the coins. They would diminish the metallic base one-half and at the same time increase the superstructure by the emission of a credit currency; or they would double the debts of the world.

THE NEW YORK TIMES.

Another leading metropolitan newspaper doubts that gold is scarce or growing scarcer, because it observes that unprecedentedly large sums of it are heaped up in the banks of England, &c., and offered in vain at low rates of interest. This critic reminds one of the pig-mies who were lost in the giant's ear: The mysterious labyrinth confused them, and being unable to take a comprehensive view of the whole subject they failed to discover that the ear was only a small appurtenance to a vast body, whose proportions were perfectly symmetrical and harmonious. It is neither the abundance nor the scarcity of money at one period compared with another that causes the rate of interest to fall or rise, but causes far different from this one.

Among these causes is the appreciation or depreciation of the standard. The reason why gold cannot find employment in England, notwithstanding it seems so plentiful in the banks, is because it is daily becoming more valuable by reason of its increasing scarcity in the markets. Nobody in England wants to borrow an ounce of gold which now costs ten days' labor while the certainty impends that he will have to pay it back with fifteen days' labor. The fact that the rate of interest is cheap is of small account to the borrower when he knows that the principal is growing dearer. Therefore he does not borrow at all, and capital defeats its own object when it seeks to grasp too much. As it is with England in respect of gold, so it is with the United States in respect of greenbacks.

FALLACIES OF MONOMETALLISTS.

The effort which you are making to unduly "appreciate" the purchasing power of these monetary units has brought all enterprises in this country to a stand-still, and capitalists seek in vain for opportunities to loan their funds even at low rates of interest. The advocates of a single standard have never seemed able to emancipate themselves from the erroneous views which were announced by the original monometallist, Sir William Petty. This gifted but erratic genius maintained that a double standard was impracticable because the market relation between the metals was liable to continual variance. The same error was maintained by John Locke and Lord Liverpool, and we find it echoed in speeches that have recently been made in this Chamber. Its origin seems to be due to the term "double standard," which conveys the notion of using both metals at the same time, whereas a double standard means nothing of the sort. It is freely admitted that however constant the relations between the metals has been and probably will continue to be throughout long periods of time, it is liable to change from the causes heretofore referred to. It is also admitted that any considerable change of this relation is sufficient to cause the melting or exportation of one metal and the importation and coinage of the other, for the two operations always occur together. It is therefore admitted to be impracticable to retain for any long time both of the metals in use to the extent of one-half each.

THE OPTIONAL STANDARD.

A double standard means not a dual standard, but an optional one. Its great advantage consists not in the maintenance of an idle, acrobatic poise between gold and silver, but in making avail of the entire stock of the two precious metals in the world as a basis of credits and of prices.

This pyramid of metallic reserve, more ancient even than that of Cheops, constitutes the basis of all prices, of all securities, of all credits, of the social relation, of property itself. You cannot get rid of it if you would. It has survived laws, theories, schemes, and plots without number, and it will continue to survive them all. The intrinsic and peculiar fitness of gold and silver respectively for money furnish the grounds of this assurance. They have the same qualities, except that one is lighter and the other is heavier, and even in this difference there is no advantage either way, for both can be handled at the same cost. You may issue a fiat of demonetization against silver, (half of this great pyramid of metal,) but you cannot destroy it. There it stands, and there it will continue to stand. Wisdom, justice, and interest counsel us to recognize this fact and to be thankful for it, and to make a proper use of it. That proper use is found in the bimetallic system or optional standard.

Having ascertained the average or pivotal point of the relation of value between the metals, which is 15¼ to 1, the bimetallic standard makes use of both of them for money, employing only one at a time, and of course the one which is temporarily cheaper at the average ratio. This cheapness is not as to other commodities, for then the change would be, in the words of the Senator from Vermont, "notably always downward." It is only between the two metals themselves, so that between them and other commodities the change may be, and was for fifteen hundred years of this era, notably always upward.

This system is not only forced upon us by its intrinsic superiority to any other; we are constrained to accept it because up to a very recent period it had been employed throughout the world for at least fifty centuries, and all the relations between man and property were based upon it and everything that it involved; and even now, although a few nations have thoughtlessly discarded it, it is still retained by nearly all the world, and those who have discarded it must adopt it again or lose their rank in the scale of civilization. The bimetallic system thus stands upon the same ground as any other of the great institutions of civilized life—intrinsic superiority and immemorial usage.

No doubt, if society could be entirely reconstructed, many of these institutions might be improved, at least so think the social reformers: but we must remember that society is of a long and gradual growth and that to cut away any of the roots by which that growth has been attained is to endanger the tree itself.

The bimetallic system has many other advantages than the organic one alluded to. For example, though theoretically only one metal is employed at a time, yet practically it employs to a large extent both metals. Coins become worn by use and the actual relation of value between a gold and silver coin in use is commonly so different from their mint relation that there would have to occur a very considerable change in the market ratio of the metals before it would pay to melt or export the coins of either one of them.

These advantages of the bimetallic standard have already been mentioned at length in my previous speech on this subject, and I do not propose to detain the Senate any longer than is necessary to set forth new matter.

Those who favor resumption in gold, being forced to acknowledge the impossibility of obtaining sufficient gold wherewith to redeem all of our Government promises to pay on demand, (to say nothing of like promises by the banks,) nevertheless hold it to be practicable to resume in gold by "appreciating" greenbacks to par in that metal. This they propose to do by contraction, that is, by retiring a portion of the emission. They scoff at greenbacks now because they are only worth 89 in gold: they call them irredeemable promises having no intrinsic value. Yet by merely diminishing their number and without being prepared to retire that number in gold, they expect to render them no longer irredeemable and to confer upon them intrinsic value. But is this possible? If greenbacks are irredeemable because they are not redeemed when quoted at 89, how can they become redeemable, if not redeemed, even when quoted at 100? If they have no intrinsic value at 89, how can they have any intrinsic value at 100? If not redeemed they must certainly continue to retain the same character they possess now. They must remain mere promises to pay, mere credit-money and exposed to all the vicissitudes of credit. The sign cannot share the nature of the thing signified. The promise can never be equal to a performance. Minus and plus are not yet convertible terms.

The main argument against the use of greenbacks or any other form of credit as money is that they have no intrinsic value. Yet the gold resumptionists do not propose to resume actually in gold. They do not propose actually to substitute gold for these intrinsically valueless pieces of paper; but, by contraction or some other means, to increase the exchangeable value of each of these paper promises of a dollar to that of a gold dollar.

INTRINSIC VALUE OF GREENBACKS.

If greenbacks have no intrinsic value when they will fetch in the market 89 in gold, will they have any intrinsic value at 90 or 95 or 100? If they are bad money because they are credit-money, when do they cease to be credit-money and when do they cease to be bad? If you have not increased the intrinsic value of the greenback, why then attempt to raise it to gold unless it be desired to give a bonus of from 13 to 20 per cent. to the creditor classes?

The fact is that greenbacks have no intrinsic value at 89 because they are merely promises to pay and a promise has no intrinsic value. Such being the case, it is impossible for them to have intrinsic value at all.

By arbitrarily contracting the emission of them or expanding the uses for them you might cause them to become worth par in gold or even more than par. You could put them at any figure you please and yet their intrinsic value would be no greater at the end than at the start. Their only value would rest upon the force of law. Withdraw that support and they would fall into the waste-paper basket. But suppose you forced them at par, would that bring the country any nearer to specie payments? Senators assume that it would ; but they fail to advance a single argument to support their assumption.

RESUMPTION OF SPECIE PAYMENTS ONLY POSSIBLE IN SILVER.

If specie payments meant simply the liquidation of the Government promises to pay on demand, we could return to specie payments to-day. We need only to offer to give 5.20 bonds for greenbacks as we did during the war and the thing could be done at once. But the fact is that resumption involves something more than merely retiring our four hundred million promises to pay. It involves the payment of the general indebtedness of the country and the means wherewith that indebtedness can be discharged. If you retire the greenbacks by funding them there would be no monetary units to replace them, and, divested of every legal means of payment except a few coins in the coffers of banks and treasuries, the only resource of the people would be repudiation ; and thus an impracticable means of bringing about specie payments would result in there being no payments at all.

In retiring the greenback you must, therefore, in order to avoid bankruptcies or distress, replace them with other monetary units, equally easy to obtain, not more easy as the expansionists would wish, because thereby you would defeat the just claims of the creditor, not less easy as the contractionists desire, because you would defeat the rights of the debtor and destroy him.

Nothing will answer for these units so well as silver dollars, because these and greenbacks are at an equality in the market and it is as easy to obtain the one as the other.

If, on the other hand, you attempt to replace the greenback with gold you will fail, because, as I have previously shown, it is difficult if not impossible to obtain sufficient gold for the purpose. If you succeed in thus replacing them, in compelling the debts of individuals and corporations to be paid in gold, you will ruin them all and plunge the country into a chronic condition of social anarchy.

THE CONFERENCE REPORT.

IN SENATE.

FRIDAY, *July* 14, 1876.

ISSUE OF SILVER COIN.

Mr. SHERMAN submitted the following report:

The committee of conference on the disagreeing votes of the two Houses on the amendments to the joint resolution (H. R. No. 109) for the issue of silver coin having met, after full and free conference have agreed to recommend, and do recommend, to their respective Houses, as follows:

That the House recede from its disagreement to the first amendment of the Senate to said joint resolution, and agree thereto amended, as follows:

In line 4 strike out the word "now" and insert "at any time."

And the Senate agree to the same.

That the Senate recede from its disagreement to the amendment of the House to the second amendment of the Senate to the said joint resolution, and agree to a substitute for said House amendment, as follows:

Add to the second amendment of the Senate the following:

SEC. 3. That in addition to the amount of subsidiary silver coin authorized by law to be issued in redemption of the fractional currency, it shall be lawful to manufacture at the several mints and issue through the Treasury and its several offices, such coin to an amount that, including the amount of subsidiary silver coin and of fractional currency outstanding, shall, in the aggregate, not exceed at any time $50,000,000.

SEC. 4. That the silver bullion required for the purposes of this act shall be purchased, from time to time, at market rate, by the Secretary of the Treasury, with any money in the Treasury not otherwise appropriated; but no purchase of bullion shall be made under this act when the market rate for the same shall be such as will not admit of the coinage and issue, as herein provided, without loss to the Treasury; and any gain or seigniorage arising from this coinage shall be accounted for and paid into the Treasury, as provided under existing laws relative to the subsidiary coinage: *Provided,* That the amount of money at any one time invested in such silver bullion, exclusive of such resulting coin, shall not exceed $200,000.

And the House agree to the same.

JOHN SHERMAN,
GEO. S. BOUTWELL,
LOUIS V. BOGY,
Managers on the part of the Senate.
H. B. PAYNE,
SAM L. J. RANDALL,
Managers on the part of the House.

Mr. JONES, of Nevada. Mr. President, I do not know why so promising a beginning should have so small an ending. I indulged the hope that the report of the committee would at least have been of such a character as to permit us to take the sense of the Senate on the transcendantly important proposition of making money, full-weighted, full legal-tender money, out of our great staple, silver; that we would have been permitted to record our votes for or against the restoration of the only legal unit of value in this country, namely, the silver dollar of the Constitution, of which we were deprived by indirection in 1874. We were deprived of it in the interest of the creditors and to the injury of the debtors of the country. But in this hope I was mistaken. I find that instead of taking any step toward the undoing of the vicious and unjust legislation of 1874, and restoring us to the same condition which we were in when specie payments were suspended—to the position we occupied when our debts were contracted—the committee have contented themselves with bringing in a bill, or rather a report, to substitute for full legal-tender paper money, debased, underweighted, subsidiary, token money to the amount of $50,000,000. In order to resume specie payments to that extent the committee would transfer the stamp of Government from the paper money, which they urge is redeemable and redeemable only in gold, to an underweighted silver token not redeemable in anything; and for this purpose they would increase the bonded indebtedness of this country, or at least take out of the sinking fund that which would decrease it if applied to that purpose. Verily, the mountain has been in labor and a mouse brought forth.

SUBSIDIARY COINAGE.

Under the present system the fractional currency is as good money, or can be exchanged for such, as any other portion of the currency. The poor man's money and the rich man's money are one as good as the other; but under the system which the committee recommends the poor man's money is good only in this country and by force of law; his scanty saving must, of necessity, be in debased token coinage; for it is in that that he will be sure to receive his wages. But the money-lender's and rich man's money will be good everywhere, needing neither Government stamp nor law to keep it up. This sort of a scheme will in no wise relieve the wants of the country or remove the pall of doubt and uncertainty which now hangs over it and causes complete stagnation and paralysis in every industrial department.

I do not see why the Government should pay out a great many millions of dollars to get a subsidiary money, when if we are not to have full-weighted money we might just as well put a stamp on paper, for it is nothing at last but a stamp on metal, and a very small amount of metal at that, compared with what it is intended to pass for. It does not meet the case at all, and I believe that the country would be infinitely better off to continue to print its fractional currency upon paper. Paper can be got, type can be got, and labor can be got from any portion of the world; but silver is scarce; it is not produced everywhere, and if we are not going to use our silver now as money, but simply to use it as a token, I think we had better continue on with our present system until necessity forces us, as it is sure to do, to use silver as full money and not subject our currency to abrasion and loss when other and cheaper material will answer for a token currency as well.

I am sorry that I have been unable, judging from the speeches that have been delivered on this floor, to make myself understood by Senators who, I am sure, are in favor of relieving the distressed condition of the business men and the laboring classes of this country. Notwithstanding this, I shall say but a few words on the subject at this time.

REPLY TO SENATOR MORTON.

The distinguished Senator from Indiana [Mr. MORTON] the other day told us that he was in favor of the silver dollar, provided you made a silver dollar that was worth a dollar. He says, "Give us a dollar that is worth a dollar, and then I am in favor of making that silver dollar a legal tender for any amount." Now the question arises what is a dollar? What does the gentleman mean by saying "worth a dollar?" We propose a silver dollar that is worth as much as any dollar that any debtor in this country owes. What other or larger silver dollar does anybody want? We propose a silver dollar that equitably liquidates obligations in this country; and this being done, what is the difference, Mr. President, as to what is the size of your unit of value?

I seems to me that—whether purposely or not I am unable to say—two questions have been mixed up with regard to the resumption of specie payments. Gentlemen tell us that we should have a standard of gold, and they tell us we must have a particular unit of that standard. The old unit in the standard of gold was 25$\frac{8}{10}$ grains of gold, nine-tenths fine. No business has been transacted upon that unit in fourteen years; no obligations have been made upon that unit in fourteen years; no notes have been drawn, no mortgages have been executed upon that unit.

Then I ask, if the paper dollar of to-day is worth only eighty-nine cents in gold, is it honest, is it right, is it legitimate, that by a trick of legislation you shall make the debtors of this country pay one hundred cents where they owe but eighty-nine? I think nobody dare answer that question in the affirmative. Gentlemen are asking for an ideal unit that has not been in existence in this country since 1861. Nobody has been doing business on the gold dollar. The people have been doing business on such a unit as the Government furnished them. I say when you resume specie payments, that is one thing; but to resume specie payments in a particular unit of a particular standard, that is an entirely different thing.

In 1834, when the business of the country was based upon silver, when all the contracts of the country were in silver, then gold was a legal tender equal with silver. At that time there were 27$\frac{1}{2}$ grains of standard gold in the dollar. When Congress attempted

4 JO

to equalize the two metals was it attempted to increase the weight of the silver dollar, which was 6¼ per cent. below the value of the gold dollar? Was it attempted at that time to raise the value of the silver dollar to the gold dollar? No, sir. Congress said it would be an outrage on the rights of the business men of the country; an outrage not to be tolerated; therefore they took one and seven-tenths grains out of the gold dollar to make it comport with the contracts and with the engagements that existed in the country.

THE UNIT OF VALUE.

There are but two classes of persons interested in what shall be the unit of value: the debtor and the creditor. To the man who owes nothing and the man who has nothing owing to him, it is not important what your unit of value shall be. If you should make two dollars out of one of the present dollars, to the man that owes nothing and has nothing owing to him all that would happen would be that he would ask twice as many dollars for what he had to sell and pay twice as many for what he had to buy.

I wonder what was the reason that in 1792 Alexander Hamilton insisted that 371¼ grains should be in the silver dollar. What a piece of stupidity it was! He must have been an old fogy to have put such an odd number of grains into a dollar—371¼ grains. Why did he not put 400 so as to admit of easy decimal relations? Why did he not put 500 or 200, so that relative calculations could be easily made? Why did he put into the dollar exactly 371¼ grains? Why did he do this when the Spanish milled dollar had 375 grains in it?

Because Hamilton knew that the unit of value made no difference to anybody but debtor and creditor, and he took the Spanish milled dollars and assayed a large number of them to find out what was the average value of that dollar and he found that 371¼ grains of pure silver was in the dollar and that 371¼ grains exactly measured the dollar that the debtor owed in this country. Hence that was the weight of the dollar ordained in 1792. He made a real dollar to exactly measure the value of the contracts in the country which had been made in dollars. He did not attempt to inflate contracts so as to agree with an ideal unit, as is proposed to be done now.

At the present time, when we have a paper dollar that is worth eighty-eight or eighty-nine cents in gold, we find a clamor made on the part of certain sections of this country that these dollars shall be "appreciated" by force of law to one hundred in gold. Sir, the gentlemen who talk so loudly of this sort of resumption are very fortunate in the fact that they find their own interest lying in the same direction with the "honor" of the Government. If you want to get to equitable specie payments, make a metal dollar that the debtor can earn with the same amount of labor as he now can earn the paper dollar which he owes, and you will have no difficulty about resumption. Do not make a dollar that gives from 15 to 25 per cent. bonus to the creditors of this country and punishes the debtors to that extent.

I predict that whenever the people of this country have a square vote on this proposition they will never submit to resumption in the present gold unit. I have been in favor of remonetizing the silver dollar because I believed that to be a preventive against the further issue of irredeemable paper money, because I believed we could the sooner and easier get to hard pan, and felt sure that the present temporary depression in silver or rise in gold must be of very short duration.

We know the cause of the so-called decline in silver; we know that Germany has not more than $150,000,000 on hand now of surplus silver to feed the world with, and we know that this country needs a great deal more than that sum to supply her wants; and if the demonetization of silver in Germany—for certainly it is not over-production, because the world is not producing more now than it did five years ago—if the demonetization has caused the appreciation of gold and decline of silver, the remonetization of silver by this country will cause silver to go back to its old normal relation with gold. It is a very easy thing, but is it a wise thing for the creditors of this Government to assist to demonetize half the money of the world and thus double its debts?

I hold it to be sound in political economy and philosophy that it is against our interest that any gold should be used as a circulating medium in this country until we have paid our debts. What an unheard-of proposition, that a country burdened with $2,000,000,000 of public debt should attempt to introduce a machine for effecting its internal exchanges that would raise the burden of such debt at least 20 per cent., and not only this, but increase also the weight of a vast amount of corporate, municipal, State, county, and city debts!

What peculiar claims have the Tweed gang upon the tax-payers of New York? When they got the bonds of that city to a large amount, they swindled the city. They did not give value to the extent of twenty cents on the dollar for the bonds that they now hold. Why should the tax-payers of New York be bound to pay these dishonestly obtained bonds in gold, when by their terms they are at best payable in paper? Why should this country, whose bonds were sold for greenbacks when greenbacks were worth but fifty cents on the coin dollar, resume specie payments in a particular metal and make those bonds good dollar for dollar in that metal and thus compel the tax-payer of this country to pay them in such particular metal? I want to know why in the resumption of specie payments every dollar of indebtedness over this broad land, which indebtedness amounts probably to $1,500,000,000 of State, county, and city indebtedness, shall be unnecessarily raised 20 per cent., and the tax-payer burdened with this unjustly increased weight of obligation?

I want to know why the seven or eight thousand millions of private debts which exist in addition to those of the nation, the States, and the municipalities, and which were engendered in greenbacks, shall be increased in the interest of the creditor and to the ruin of the debtor. I tell you, sir, it is not the money-lender that gives prosperity to the country; it is the active business man; it is the borrower, the hopeful, the industrious, the enterprising man; he who is always in debt. That is the man who lends fleetness to the wings of commerce; that is the man who gives elasticity to the flagging footsteps of industry. It is not the man who, instead of inaugurating enterprises, sits back and lends money. If any legislation is to be had, it should be in favor of the masses of the people of the country. Let a few honest words be said for Lazarus; let us not always be nodding to Dives. We hear a wail throughout this country from certain classes whenever you propose to make money plenty so as to keep up prices at the range in which they were when debts were contracted. We hear a wail lest somebody with a fixed income is going to be hurt, or somebody with a fixed salary is going to be hurt. We have heard no words of encouragement or defense for that much larger class who have incomes neither fixed nor unfixed, but who have very fixed obligations to meet.

I have already said more than I intended to when I arose. I did not intend to go further than to protest against the smothering of this great question by the action of the conference committee so that a fair vote of the Senate cannot be had upon it.

We now come to the proposition of issuing subsidiary coin, something foreign to the bill that we thought we were going to discuss, and upon whose merits we can get no vote because many gentlemen in this Chamber who are in favor of issuing a full-weighted silver dollar are also in favor of this proposition of subsidiary coins. I should have liked a vote taken so that the people of this country could know who it is that is in favor of inflation; I mean that worse kind of inflation, the inflation of debts and a contraction in the prices of property and labor. That is the inflation which the people ought to dread the most.

I desire to call the attention of the Senate to the following points in this connection:

RECAPITULATION OF CERTAIN POINTS.

First. I would warn the Senate of the serious juncture of business affairs throughout the country.

No remedy exists for this state of affairs but that of giving the country such a unit of value as will encourage bank discounts, render the money market easy, and enable debtors and mortgagors to equitably liquidate their indebtedness. Such a unit of value is only to be found in the silver dollar.

Second. That the present time is the best for the application of this remedy. Gold has risen, and with it the greenbacks, which, owing to a perversion of the law, are now based upon gold. I say that gold and greenbacks have risen so high that the latter will purchase in the market enough silver to render possible the resumption of specie payments in silver. The accomplishment of this result would put an end to the existing fall of prices and tightness of loanable funds. Let the present opportunity pass and it may never again be in our power to recall it.

Third. That, in order to consolidate her recently-established unity, Germany has resolved to call in the numerous silver coins of her component states and issue gold coins instead. Her efforts to carry out this policy, which, whatever may be its wisdom from a political or dynastic point of view, is financially unsound and dangerous, has caused a rapid rise in gold and fall in silver. The nature of this perturbation in the long-standing relation between the metals is such that it can only be temporary. *While it is our last opportunity.* No other country except the United States is in a position to take Germany's rejected stock of silver; specie payments having been suspended in many of the countries of Europe. We know exactly how much silver Germany has to sell. We know exactly how much we need in order to resume specie payments and with it our lost commercial prosperity. The two amounts are substantially the same; so that if we absorb Germany's stock, the price of silver will rise and gold will fall, until the old-time relation will be restored. Why, then, shall we refuse to seize this propitious moment and refuse to make avail of the advantages it offers us?

Fourth. I have said that the present abnormal enhancement of gold and depression of silver can only be for a time, but unless we put a stop to it at once by removing the restraints imposed by the sinister legislation of 1873, a great revulsion will be brought upon the country. A new and further expansion of paper will occur. Either this or repudiation will be the only choice left us. And the evil may not stop here. You propose to consummate an act of great injustice upon a free people, and I warn you that it is not to be done with impunity. Our forefathers revolted from authority rather than pay an enhanced price for a few chests of tea. Now you would assist to impose an addition of 20 per cent. to all the debts of this country, and I do not believe that the spirit of liberty is so dead with our people that you will succeed in accomplishing this purpose without opposition. You are treading upon dangerous ground. You are pressing the spring down too far.

Fifth. To arrest the present rise of gold and fall of silver will be to save the country from numberless sacrifices and dangers. To refuse to do it will invite new difficulties and disorders. It is in your power to adopt either course. Upon you lies the grave responsibility of deciding this important subject correctly.

Sixth. The country will hold us to a strict accountability and the votes on this subject will be scrutinized with more severity six months hence than on any other subject.

Seventh. Before this Congress meets again the opportunity to purchase silver at 20 per cent. under gold will be lost. The opportunity to resume payments in specie will be lost. The opportunity to relieve the commercial dread and uncertainty which now tie the hands of industry will be lost.

Eighth. There are other grave dangers with which inaction on this subject menaces us. Our fisheries, the whole product of which is valued at but a few millions a year, have always formed an important subject of legislation with us. It forms the basis of many of our foreign treaties. It has often drawn us into controversies which threatened the country with war. And yet how insignificant are not all of the New England fisheries compared with the Pacific coast mines. The product of these mines amounts to over a hundred millions a year. They form the basis of the industries of several important States. They support directly and indirectly several millions of persons. Their product is indispensable to the world and forms an indissoluble portion of its industries. Yet you propose to destroy them all by adverse legislation or inaction. Is this a wise or just course?

Ninth. If you fail to restore the silver dollar to its rank of full legal tender, and so neglect the mining interests of the country, the mines will be closed and all the capital invested in the veins of the Sierra Nevadas will be lost. At one blow you will destroy hundreds of millions, and to the industrial distress that already exists in the East you will add that of the far West. The mines, once abandoned, will never be re-opened. If neglected for six months the restoration of the old normal market relation of 16 to 1 will not be sufficient to induce their re-opening.

Tenth. Nature has given us the vast range of the Sierra Nevadas rich with argentiferous deposits. That which the world has sighed for fifty centuries to grasp and in quest of which this continent was drenched in blood by its Spanish conquerors, nature has given us in reward for scientific and enlightened labor. But no sooner do we come into possession of the coveted prize than you would deprive us of it by legislation.

Eleventh. We have protected everything in our laws except the precious metals. Codfish, bodkins, shoe-strings, and tombstones are protected; even iron, steel, nickel, and copper are protected; but not gold and silver. These great metals which differ from all other substances in the most important respect that there is a vast stock of them on hand in the world stored up from the ages, these bases of contracts, these conservators of prices, of the relations between capital and labor, of property, of civilization, these we do not protect at all. More than this, we propose to destroy that one of them which we produce in the greatest abundance and to adopt the one which Great Britain almost monopolizes.

Twelfth. The trade of Asia lies at our doors. Instead of opening these doors to it, we propose to double lock and bolt them. By assisting to lower the purchasing power of silver we deny ourselves all the profits of this great commerce.

Thirteenth. You will render almost valueless a vast portion of our possessions stretching from Mexico to Alaska. Adding to this' your one-sided taxes on iron, steel, tools, chemicals, and the numerous other commodities employed in the production of silver, you will cause great discontent among the people of the Pacific coast States, and induce them to believe that they are denied that equal protection and encouragement which they are entitled to under the terms of the Constitution.

Fourteenth. The size of a unit of value is of no account except between debtors and creditors. Give these a unit which accurately measures the contracts between them and you do justice to both. This is what was done in 1792 by adopting the silver dollar. This is what would be done by adopting it now. No man would complain and the country would enjoy an immense relief.

Fifteenth. Subsidiary coins are only tokens representing gold. Substantially they are promises to pay gold printed on silver. They had better be printed on paper; it is cheaper.

Sixteenth. The error which lies at the base of all erroneous views on this subject is the supposition that gold is immovable. But this is fallacious. Gold is subject to the same laws of supply and demand as other commodities. It rises and falls just the same. This fact is discernible whenever it is valued in any other commodity than itself. Whatever there seems to be of fixity about gold applies with even greater force to silver, because its production and consumption are more regular. The assumed immobility of gold reminds one of the geocentric theory of the universe, which theory assumed the earth to be stationary and all the planets and the sun to revolve around it; whereas we now know that the earth revolves around the sun and the sun itself around some more distant center.

The question before us is too important to be buried beneath a puerility like this error. We must settle it with all our eyes open or we will bring upon the country such an aggravation of distress, and that quickly too, that no man can foresee in what dire disasters it will end.

Seventeenth. It is claimed that the issue of token coins under the bill now before us will be a step toward the resumption of specie payments in the East. I maintain that, on the contrary, it is a step toward the suspension of specie payments in the West. The Pacific coast States, California, Nevada, Oregon, and some of the Territories, and to some extent also the State of Texas, have a specie currency and have never suspended specie payments. This currency, according to the custom of the country and under the law as at present construed, is of gold. In this state of affairs the Government, under the act of 1853, issued several millions of silver tokens which were sent to these States and put into circulation, the Government receiving for them their nominal or tale value in gold, thus making some 10 or 15 per cent. by the operation and flooding those States with a large amount of subsidiary coins.

After having done this, the Government under the present bill will turn right around and sell this same sort of subsidiary coin to the Eastern States for par in greenbacks. The Pacific States took this coin and gave gold for it, with the understanding, derived from the law as it then stood, and relying upon the good faith of the Government, that none of it would be issued except for gold. But, in violation of this faith and after you sold all you could for gold, you sell the same coin in the East for greenbacks, which are at 12 per cent. discount in gold. At the present time a man in California can sell a gold dollar for $1.12 in greenbacks and buy $1.12 in subsidiary silver coins, which the law makes him to pay out at par in California. By compelling the Pacific States to pay you gold for what you are now selling for greenbacks you wronged them out of some $600,000. By now issuing fifty millions more of this token coinage you will compel them to suspend specie payments. Already your token coins are at a discount of 6 per cent. in San Francisco, and this depreciation will be aggravated by the present bill. You have in effect left that coast without any par fractional currency for their gold coins. This anomalous state of affairs has produced an extraordinary derangement of the currency. Wholesale prices are quoted in gold and retail prices in debased silver. There can be but one ending to this. That ending will be suspension. The Pacific coast community must have small coins, and the value of those coins must be in accord with the larger ones. The former cannot be repudiated, because there must be a fractional currency, and there is no way of replacing the debased coins. Our banks cannot issue fractional notes. But gold will cease to be paid. This means suspension of specie payments and the exportation of some thirty millions of gold from the country.

Yet the legislation which is responsible for it is by some erroneously styled and by others complacently regarded as "a step toward specie payments!"

The PRESIDENT *pro tempore*. The question is on concurring in the report of the committee of conference.

The report was concurred in.

www.ingramcontent.com/pod-product-compliance
Lightning Source LLC
Chambersburg PA
CBHW021639270326
41931CB00008B/1091